Recipes from

WHAT'S COOKING

with

RUTH FREMES
Volume Two

 METHUEN

Toronto   New York   London   Sydney   Auckland

Canadian Cataloguing in Publication Data

Fremes, Ruth, 1930–
    Recipes from What's cooking with Ruth Fremes

Collection of recipes from the author's television
program What's cooking with Ruth Fremes.
Includes index.
ISBN 0-458-94640-0 (v.1). -- ISBN 0-458-95180-3 (v.2)

1. Cookery.   I. What's cooking with Ruth Fremes
(Television program)   II. Title.

TX715.F73   641.5   C80-094824-6

Printed and bound in Canada
1 2 3 4 5   81   86 85 84 83 82

CONTENTS

FOREWORD

My idea of a superwoman is Ruth Fremes. She is also my idea of a tyrant because when you appear on her television show "What's Cooking" nothing but the best will do for her viewers. Her standard of excellence is extremely high and she insists on it without mercy. Somehow this is fun. I have actually refused to appear on the Merv Griffin Show and on Phil Donahue's show because Ruth had booked me first.

What the viewers watching "What's Cooking" don't see is the fantastic rush forward by everyone else in the studio the moment we're off the air. The technicians and cameramen are anxious to taste the tempting dishes that Ruth has prepared on the show.

In her writing Ruth Fremes is informative and efficient. She is so careful in the selection of her recipes that those which finally appear in her cookbook are, so to speak, only the tip of the iceberg: any that are not outstanding after having been tested in her kitchen are thrown out without hesitation by Ruth.

I hope this book is a failure. Why? Because then Ruth will have to get back where she belongs—cooking in her own kitchen for her friends. But, of course, she has loads of friends, some of whom she hasn't met yet. It is tedious to walk along a Canadian city street with Ruth Fremes since she is stopped repeatedly on the sidewalk and in shops by fans asking for her autograph. She is held in such affection by those who meet her for the first time that old friends, such as myself, realize we just can't keep Ruth to ourselves—now the secret is out!

What's the secret? Ruth Fremes alone, unaided and almost without effort, will transform *you* into a superlative cook!

Shirley Conran
Author of *Superwoman*

INTRODUCTION

The fourth season of "What's Cooking" is about to begin. During the past year I have searched for, tested, weeded through, discarded and finally chosen recipes that I believe you'll like. They had to be interesting because I know you like to watch "What's Cooking" for the technique as much as for the meal ideas. They had to be nutritious, simple to prepare, reasonable in price, and delicious to eat. With a few exceptions—Coulibiac could hardly be called simple or reasonable; Chocolate Decadence could never be called nutritious—I think this collection fills the bill. Each recipe was tried several times and a great many of them have found their way into my all-time favorite recipe file. I hope they are as attractive to you.

There are some new features in this year's book. A new section, *Breads and Baked Savories* provides recipes for special breads and casseroles. Spanish Chicken is a spicy chicken and hot sausage mixture that is prepared in a special brioche. These dishes are spectacular to serve to guests; the fillings are tasty, either by themselves or served on hot toasts or in pita bread.

Meatless Main Dishes is another new section which includes recipes for dishes served as whole meals without fish, meat or poultry. Some of our favorites are there.

I've also tried to answer your questions in sections of the book where the answers would be most useful.

Again, I wish to thank you all for your encouragement and support for "What's Cooking." My thanks go to the television crew and staff who make this all happen, to make-up artists Pat, Jennifer, Helen, Brenda, Barbara and Hilary who ensure that the steamer doesn't turn my hair limp and make my mascara drip. And for Barb, Gerry, Elena and Anne for making the food ever so perfect when I spill the beans, literally!

Fondest wishes and bon appetit!

A Few Words About Blended Butter

Many of the recipes in this volume use blended butter as an ingredient. Blended butter is simply a form of homemade spread, designed to balance the saturated fat in butter with the polyunsaturated fat from oil. If your doctor has recommended that you decrease your saturated fat intake and use margarine instead, you may find this blend of butter and oil a tasty alternative. Any of the recipes in this book can use butter, margarine or blended butter satisfactorily.

Ingredients

- 2 tablespoons powdered skim milk
- ⅔ cup safflower oil (if unavailable use sunflower or corn or soybean oil)
- ¼ pound butter at room temperature

Method

Combine powdered skim milk and oil in blender jar or large bowl. Leave for 5 minutes. Blend with motor at low speed. If beating by hand, add oil gradually, beating well after each addition. Add softened butter and continue blending until smooth. Put into covered container and refrigerate. (If you wish, you can use more oil but you'll have to store it in the freezer.)

IF YOU'RE COOKING FOR ONE OR TWO

Here is a list of recipes that may be whizzed from stove to table without mathematics or extra preparation.

Soup:	Dieter's ratatouille soup
Main course:	Crisp broiled chicken breast
	Chicken livers with vegetables
	Quick chick
	Stuffed acorn squash
	Lamb fricassee
	Kidney and mushroom casserole
	Supper-on-the-run
Vegetables:	Any fresh or frozen vegetable may be steamed, either alone or in combination
Salad:	Check the list of salad dressings for raw or cooked vegetables
Dessert:	Quick apple crisp

A FEW WORDS ABOUT HERBS AND SPICES

- Many fresh herbs can grow in pots near your kitchen window or in window boxes. Plant seeds in the late winter or early spring and keep the soil just moist.

- Fresh herbs such as dill, parsley, chives or basil can be kept in near-fresh condition if you wash them, shake them well, and put them in tightly closed glass jars in the refrigerator. (Fresh rosemary will keep in a glass of water in the kitchen for 2 weeks or more if the water is changed daily).

- Practically all fresh herbs can be frozen if wrapped airtight. Their fresh green color won't disappear if they are used straight from the freezer, without thawing.

- When you double a recipe, do not double the amount of herbs or spices. Use just a little more than called for in the original recipe.

- Dried herbs will bring more flavor to food if they are crushed or crumbled well between your palms as you add them to the cooking. This releases the bouquet.

List of Seasonings

Basil. Use in soups, meat, cereals and sauces. Also in French-style kidneys.

Bay Laurel. Use in soups, roast meat, stews and various sauces. Also in beef fillets, meatballs, mixed liver, stuffed rolled bacon.

Caraway. Crush caraway seeds by pounding them with a hammer covered with a tea towel or by placing them in a blender. Add to a meat or vegetable sauce for a pleasant flavor.

Chives. To grow chives in your kitchen, buy a small pot from the vegetable market and transplant to a larger one with more soil and a drainage hole in the bottom. Water only enough to keep the soil moist. They'll grow for months if kept in the light.

The best way to cut chives is with small kitchen scissors. Cut them off at the top of the plant and the plant will keep growing.

To freeze, wash the stems well and shake vigorously. Then put them in waxed paper, plastic wrap or a tightly capped jar and store in the freezer. They'll keep their green color if used immediately, before defrosted.

Cinnamon. Place 2 or 3 sticks of cinnamon in a jar and cover with sugar. Screw the cap on tightly and let stand for a few weeks. Use in cakes, tea or coffee. (You can add vanilla pods to this.) Replace the sugar as you use it, shake the jar well and return to the shelf.

Mix sugar and powdered cinnamon and keep the mixture in a jar (1 teaspoon of cinnamon to 2 tablespoons of sugar). In the store, this mixture costs three times the price of making it yourself.

Curry. Curry powders differ so much that the safest rule to follow is to use half the amount of curry powder or paste called for in a recipe. You can always add more to taste before serving.

Spice things up a bit by adding 1 teaspoonful (or more) of curry powder to biscuit dough, bread dough, dumplings, salad dressing or cottage cheese.

Dill. To freeze fresh dill, first wash and hang it upside down to dry. Then wrap in waxed paper or plastic wrap and freeze. Use straight from freezer.

Dry your own dill for much less than it costs to buy dried. Cut fresh dill into small bits with scissors and then spread on a cookie sheet covered with some paper towelling. Either let dry at room temperature (stirring now and then) for a couple of days, or put in a low, low oven. Stir from time to time. Then put in a tightly covered jar. If the oven is low enough, the dill will keep its green color.

The dill you buy to use in pickling must be mature, not young feathery dill. Ask for dill which has just gone to seed. Young dill (the kind that's used for salads) won't give pickles the right flavor.

Use scissors to cut feathery dill tips into cream sauces served with fish or vegetables. Also add them to leafy green salads for a fresh garden flavor. Use a lot of fresh dill in a hot vegetable soup.

Ginger. One tablespoon of raw ginger (bought in a fruit and vegetable or Oriental food store) equals ½ teaspoon of powdered ginger in strength.

Add thin slices of candied ginger to meat, fish and chicken dishes. It's also marvelous in curries and sweet and sour sauces for tongue, for example.

Marjoram. Use in soups, roast meat and sauces. Also in rice salad, rice with sauce.

Mustard. To make a good prepared mustard at home, mix dry, powdered mustard with enough cool water to make a smooth paste. Add a little salt and other flavorings such as tumeric. Let it stand about 10 minutes to reach full flavor. Mustard prepared in this way is pungent and tasty, but unfortunately begins to lose strength after about 1 hour. Don't bother to save what's left. Make a fresh batch each time you need it.

Nutmeg. An average nutmeg will produce about 3 teaspoons grated. Ready-ground nutmeg is flavorful, but it doesn't have the zing of freshly ground. Buy nutmegs whole and grate them into batter or on top of creamed dishes and custards. Add some grated nutmeg to puréed spinach.

Oregano. Use for pizza, meat with tomatoes and various tomato sauces. Also in marrow with tomatoes, stewed rabbit, mixed liver.

Paprika. Paprika can be used with chicken, meat or fish recipes, as well as sprinkled on many vegetables, salads and creamed dishes. It gives a rich color and flavor to soups, stews and rice.

Use plenty of paprika when you make pot roasts. It not only adds incomparably to the taste but it also gives a beautifully colored gravy.

Parsley. Keep parsley fresh by placing it stem-side down in a jar with a little cold water—not enough to reach the leaves. Screw on the top and refrigerate. This will keep nicely for several days.

Parsley freezes very well. Wash, shake and hang to dry, then cut off the leaf heads and put them in the freezer in a covered jar or plastic container. If parsley has been well dried before freezing, it will crush into fine flakes if the frozen leaf heads are rubbed vigorously between the palms. The color and flavor keep excellently.

Parsley will chop very finely if it is thoroughly dried with a tea towel before cut; otherwise, the pieces will stick together and not disperse into fine flakes.

Rosemary. Use in soups, roast potatoes and various sauces. Also in pork with cheese, mixed liver, rice with sauce.

Sage. Use for game, various sauces and turkey dressing. Also in hot spiced chicken, tomatoes in the mold, rolled stuffed bacon.

Thyme. Use in soups and various sauces. Also in tomatoes in the mold, stewed rabbit, turkey wings with olive leaves.

HORS D'OEUVRES AND APPETIZERS

Bagna Cauda

Bagna Cauda is a country dish which originated in the farm kitchens of northern Italy. Transported to the living rooms of North America it has become a sophisticated hors d'oeuvre with the bite of hot garlic and the flavor of sweet, crisp, chilled vegetables. We love it! (Serves 6)

Cold Dipping Vegetables (any, some or all of the following)

Sweet red peppers
Green peppers
Carrots, medium-sized
Cucumbers, peeled and seeded
Green onions, young
Stalks of celery

Broccoli pieces
Cauliflower flowerettes
Turnip
Mushrooms
Asparagus tips
Radishes

Bread sticks

Hot Dipping Sauce

2   cups heavy cream
4   cloves garlic, peeled and pierced with a toothpick
4   tablespoons unsalted butter

8   flat, canned anchovy fillets, finely chopped
$\frac{1}{8}$ teaspoon cayenne

Method

Clean and cut all the vegetables, except the green onions, into 2- or 3-inch lengths about $\frac{1}{2}$ inch wide. Soak them in a bowl of ice water for at least one hour until very crisp. Then dry with paper towels, arrange them on a platter, and refrigerate covered until ready to serve.

Bring cream and the cloves of garlic to a boil in a small, heavy saucepan. Let the cream boil rather briskly until it shows signs of thickening, then turn down the heat and stir almost constantly with a wooden spoon until the cream measures just 1 cupful. Pour it into a cup or small bowl and let cool. Remove garlic.

Meanwhile, in a clean saucepan, melt butter over low heat and add the chopped anchovies. Watch that the butter does not turn brown. Stir in the reduced cream, sprinkle with cayenne, and heat the sauce *almost* to the boiling point.

The best dish in which to serve the Bagna Cauda is a small earthenware or enamel casserole in which it can be kept hot, without boiling, over a candle warmer or electric hot tray. Dip in the cold vegetables or bread sticks and provide plenty of napkins!

Blue Cheese Toasts

Delightful companion to soups, but good enough to serve as hot canapes. (Serves 6–8)

Ingredients

3	ounces cottage cheese	6–8	slices pumpernickel or rye bread, toasted
2	ounces Roquefort or Blue cheese		

Method

Cream cheeses together until softened and light. Spread on toasted bread. Broil briefly, until tops are bubbly and lightly browned.

Note: If you prefer a milder Blue cheese flavor, reduce Blue cheese to 1 ounce.

Chicken Liver Spread

When I first sampled this creamy spread at a friend's house, I marvelled at the consistency and flavor. Since using the recipe myself, I am convinced that it would be difficult to make a pâté that surpasses it. If it is prepared in advance, cover it with a layer of melted butter or shortening and refrigerate. Toss out the congealed fat before serving, of course. It can be frozen and will keep for up to 3 weeks. (Makes 1 pound or approximately 2½ cups)

Ingredients

½	pound or 1 cup butter	¼	cup apple brandy (Calvados) or apple cider
½	cup chopped onions		
2	tablespoons chopped shallots	2–4	tablespoons 18% cream
		1	teaspoon lemon juice
1	medium apple, such as Greening or Macintosh	1½	teaspoons salt
			Pinch freshly ground black pepper
1	pound chicken livers, cleaned and halved		

Method

Cut the butter in half and leave aside ½ cup to soften. Put half the remaining portion (¼ cup) in a frypan and melt. Add the onions and shallots and allow them to soften over medium heat, stirring every so often for an even color. Peel the apple, seed and chop it. The apple should be tart—it will give the pâté its mellow flavor. Add the apple and cook for about 4 minutes or until everything is soft. Remove to a blender or food processor and leave until the livers are done.

Add another ¼ cup butter to the frypan, the clean livers and sauté over high heat, turning often with a wooden spoon. When they are well browned but still underdone inside, remove from the heat. Flame the pan with the brandy or cider. To do this, warm the brandy in a small pan until hot. Pour over the hot livers and quickly light with a match, away from the heat. Allow the flame to disappear completely. Now, add this mixture to the onion-apple mixture and process. Add the cream to thin it down, if necessary. Cover and allow to cool.

Now, back to the other ½ cup of butter. It should be just ready for hand beating. Beat it with a wooden spoon until it reaches the texture of whipped butter, then add and blend the liver mixture into it. If the butter is too hard chunks of it will remain throughout; if it is too soft, it will be oily. Now, add the lemon juice, salt and pepper. Taste and adjust seasonings, if necessary.

Place pâté in an attractive crock and refrigerate until quite cold. Serve with melba crackers, cocktail rye bread or crisp vegetables.

Cucumber-Yogurt Dip

Here's a refreshing dip to whet appetites before dinner. Serve with raw sliced vegetables. (Makes 2 cups)

Ingredients

2	cups plain yogurt	1	teaspoon finely chopped mint
1	tablespoon light vegetable oil	1	small clove garlic, crushed
2	teaspoons lemon juice	1	large cucumber, peeled and finely grated
	Pinch of salt		

Method

Combine yogurt, oil, lemon juice, salt, mint, and garlic. Add grated cucumber, stir well and chill before serving.

Now that I have discovered natural yogurt, I can't seem to use it enough. Have you any new ideas?
Try the No Egg Carrot Cake (p. 111), Broccoli and Apple Soup (p. 15), Cucumber and Spinach Soup (p. 23), Iced Sorrel Soup (p. 24), Chilly Tomato Bisque (p. 24), Burger Stroganoff (p. 26), Apple Yogurt Dessert (p. 123), or Icy Yogurt Pops (p. 126).

Tapanade

This vegetable dip from southern France is redolent of garlic. Its origin is clear—from the coast of the Mediterranean where olives and anchovies thrive. Served with fresh vegetables kept crisp in ice water, this dip is a favorite for cocktail parties. (Makes about 2 cups)

Ingredients

3   cans (50 grams each) flat anchovy fillets, washed with cool water and drained

1   6½-ounce (189 mL) can tuna fish, washed in cool water and drained

1   cup pitted, black, Greek olives

2   tablespoons capers, drained

3   medium cloves garlic, chopped

⅓   cup lemon juice

¼   cup olive oil

Freshly ground pepper (optional)

Method

If a less salty dip is desired, place the tuna fish and anchovies in a wire sieve and pour boiling water through. Combine all ingredients except the oil in a food processor with the steel knife attachment. A blender may also be used. Process until smooth. With the motor running, add the oil in a thin stream. Taste. Add black pepper for more zing. Chill covered until ready to serve.

To make a tapanade without an electric kitchen aid, simply chop everything well, combine in a large bowl and beat with a wooden spoon. In France, this tapanade usually is prepared by hand, using a marble bowl and a blunt mallet. When the mixture reaches the proper consistency, add oil gradually and season with pepper. Traditionally the dip is served at room temperature, but chill, if desired.

Spicy Bean Dip

A hearty dip, perfect for football weather! Serve hot with tortilla chips. (Makes 1½ cups)

Ingredients

1   14- or 19-ounce (398 mL or 540 mL) can pinto beans

1   clove garlic, minced

2   tablespoons hot green chilies, chopped

1   tablespoon Worcestershire sauce

6   drops hot pepper sauce

Pinch ground cumin

Method

Drain pinto beans, reserving liquid. Mash beans and heat in saucepan with remaining ingredients and about 3 tablespoons reserved bean liquid, over low heat.

Guacamole

This Mexican dish has its own distinctive fine flavor. It tastes best if made just before serving. Scoop up with tortilla chips. (Makes 1 cup)

Ingredients

1	small onion	2	tablespoons lemon juice
1	clove garlic, peeled	2	serrano chilies or any other fresh hot green chilies, finely chopped
2	avocados, ripe, peeled and seeded		
1	tomato, medium-sized, peeled and seeded		

Method

In food processor (with steel blade attachment) or blender, process onion and garlic until minced. Add remaining ingredients and blend until desired consistency is reached.

Ham and Chutney Dip

A delicate blend of flavors for nibbling at a party. Crisp raw vegetable slices can replace crackers as the "dipper." (Makes about 1½ cups)

Ingredients

½	pound ham, cooked and chopped	3	tablespoons minced chutney
½	cup mayonnaise	1½	teaspoons curry powder
½	cup sour cream	½	teaspoon lemon juice
⅓	cup tinned water chestnuts, chopped		Cayenne
			Salt, if desired

Method

Chop the ham into very fine pieces. Combine with the rest of the ingredients. Blend well and cover. Refrigerate until serving time.

Seviche of Scallops

Seviche is an appetizer that is usually prepared from a combination of raw, salt-water fish. It is served in such countries as Japan and the Caribbean. The fish is "cooked" for several hours in lime juice marinade. This version uses scallops only and is very delicate. It should not marinate for more than 4 hours as the mixture will become too liquid. Plan to prepare this dish 3 hours before serving. (Serves 4)

Ingredients

¾ pound scallops

½ cup lime juice, approximately 6 medium limes, juiced

2 tablespoons chopped green onion

2 tablespoons chopped Italian or Chinese parsley

1 medium tomato, peeled, seeded and chopped (see p. 97)

1 small clove garlic, peeled and well chopped

1 small avocado, peeled and cut into 8 sections

¼ cup olive oil

½ teaspoon salt

½ teaspoon freshly ground black pepper

Dash Tabasco sauce

Method

Wash, dry and cut the scallops into quarters, and lay in a low dish that can accommodate them in a single layer. Pour the lime juice over top. Refrigerate for 1 hour. Meanwhile, prepare the vegetables (except the avocado which will turn brown) and mix the dressing of oil, salt, pepper and Tabasco. After the marinating period, the scallops will be firm-fleshed and have changed from their original translucence to a white color. Just before serving combine the fish with the onion, parsley, garlic, tomato and dressing. Toss gently to mix.

Serve on plates or in goblets and garnish with the peeled avocado. Return to the refrigerator for chilling for about ½ hour.

Tomato-Cheese Croustades

Prepare these croustades ahead of time, then toast and make the filling. Fill and bake when the first guest rings the doorbell. (Serves 12)

Ingredients

3-inch round cookie cutter

12 slices white bread, thinly sliced

1 small tomato, peeled, seeded and chopped (see p. 97)

1 teaspoon fresh basil, chopped

½ teaspoon salt

Black pepper, freshly ground

¼ cup Gruyère cheese, grated

Butter

Method

Preheat oven to 400°F. Cut a round from each slice of bread with a cookie cutter. Fit the rounds into tiny buttered muffin tins, molding them gently to form little cups. Bake in the middle of the oven for 10–12 minutes, until golden.

Peel, seed and coarsely chop tomato. In a small bowl combine tomato with basil, salt and black pepper. Taste for seasoning. Fill each croustade with 1 teaspoon grated Gruyère cheese and spread about ½ teaspoon tomato mixture on top. Then dot with butter.

To bake, preheat oven to 350°F. Arrange croustades on a baking dish, or jelly-roll pan, and bake about 10 minutes. Slide under the broiler for a few seconds to brown the tops and serve hot.

Spinach Croustades

Here is a splendid croustade sent to us from San Francisco's Tante Marie. (Serves 12)

Ingredients

1 3-inch round cookie cutter	1 tablespoon butter
12 slices white bread, thinly sliced	1 tablespoon shallots, minced
	¼ cup grated Gruyère cheese
2 cups fresh spinach leaves or ½ cup cooked, drained and chopped	Butter
	Red pepper
Salt	

Method

Preheat oven to 400°F. With cookie cutter, cut a round from each slice of white bread. Fit rounds into tiny buttered muffin tins, molding them gently to form little cups. Bake them in the middle of the oven for 10–12 minutes until golden.

Wash and stem fresh spinach and cook in a heavy-bottomed pot with a little salt. Keep turning until all the leaves are wilted. When cooked, remove and squeeze dry and chop. Put butter and shallots into the pan and cook until soft. Add the chopped spinach and cook until most of the water has evaporated.

Fill each croustade with 1 teaspoon of the cheese and spread about ½ teaspoon spinach mixture on top. Then dot with butter. Arrange croustades on a baking dish or jelly-roll pan, and bake about 10 minutes at 350°F. Slide under the broiler for a few seconds to brown the tops, then decorate with a little red pepper. Serve hot.

SOUPS

HOT SOUPS
Broccoli and Apple Soup 15
Chicken Broth 16
Quick Vegetable Soup 17
Tuscan Minestrone 18
Cream of Pumpkin Soup 19
Tomato Soup Portugaise 20
Sweet Potato Soup 21
Crockpot Potato-Leek Chowder 21
Beet Borscht 22

COLD SOUPS
Dieter's Ratatouille Soup 22
Cold Cucumber and Spinach Soup 23
Iced Sorrel Soup 24
Chilly Tomato Bisque 24

Broccoli and Apple Soup

Vegetarians will quickly recognize the new taste combination in this pale green soup. It's attractive for dinner parties because of the subtlety of its colors and because it can be prepared in advance and reheated after the guests have arrived.

A word of warning! Taste the soup before adding any salt. Salt quickly disguises the taste of apple which distinguishes this soup. (Serves 4–6)

Ingredients

1	bunch broccoli		Salt
3	tablespoons butter		Freshly ground pepper
1	small onion, thinly sliced	4	tablespoons crème fraîche,
1	apple, peeled, cored and		sour cream, or yogurt
	roughly diced		(optional)
4	cups water or chicken stock		
2	tablespoons minced chives, or parsley		

Method

Separate broccoli flowers and trim 2 inches from the stalks. Peel outer skin with a vegetable peeler. Dice stalks and flowers.

Melt butter in a 4-quart saucepan. Add onion and apple, cover and cook over low heat for 10 minutes. Add broccoli, stock or water. Bring to a boil and simmer, covered, over medium heat for 30 minutes. Remove the soup from the heat. Transfer ⅓ to a blender or food processor, and mix until smooth. Repeat in 2 more batches. Reheat the soup, stirring constantly. Taste and add seasoning. Serve with sour cream, crème fraîche, or yogurt.

Can I substitute yogurt for sour cream in all my cooking?
Yes, with adjustments. Yogurt is more liquid and more tart. For desserts and salads use them interchangeably. For baking, when the recipe calls for sour cream you can use 1 cup yogurt but *add* 2 tablespoons of vegetable oil and *subtract* 2 tablespoons of liquid. For sauces add 1 or 2 tablespoons of corn starch and cook over very low heat for a short time. Add room temperature yogurt at the very last minute of cooking when making stroganoff or casseroles on top of the stove.

Chicken Broth

There are as many ways of making chicken broth as there are cooks. The Chinese use thin slices of ginger, Europeans use onions with the skins, and New Yorkers suggest sprigs of fresh dill. Each has a different taste, so choose a recipe for the end result you prefer—a thick, rich-flavored broth; a light, sparkling one; or simply a tender chicken for salad. Here is a basic recipe with variations and suggestions for using the chicken. (Makes about 3 quarts)

Ingredients

4–5	pound whole chicken, washed	10	whole peppercorns
2	cloves unpeeled garlic	1	tablespoon salt
		4	quarts cold water, approximately
	Bouquet consisting of 6 sprigs parsley and a small bay leaf, tied together	1	teaspoon thyme

Optional

1	veal knuckle, cut up and cracked	3	stalks celery and their leaves
2	medium onions, peeled and halved	1	2-inch slice each of turnip and parsnip
1	large carrot, cut into 3-inch chunks		

Method

In a large stock pot, combine all the above ingredients except the thyme. Add the 4 quarts of water last and, if the fowl isn't quite covered, add a little more. Over high heat, bring the water to a boil and, with a slotted spoon or skimmer, thoroughly skim off all the scum as it rises to the surface. Reduce the heat so that the liquid barely moves, add the thyme, and simmer, half covered, for at least 4 hours. Remove the chicken and the veal bones, and strain the finished stock through a fine sieve. If it is to be used at once, let it rest a few moments, then with a large spoon skim off as much of the surface fat as you can. If the flavor of the stock isn't intense enough at this point, return it to the heat and boil it rapidly until it becomes more concentrated. Refrigerate it uncovered.

This stock will keep in the refrigerator about 3 days, possibly 4; at that point, either bring it to a boil and refrigerate it again for the same length of time, or freeze it in small quantities to be used as required. Make it a practice to save and freeze such bits of an uncooked, cut-up chicken as the wing-tips, gizzard, heart, and neck. Add them, without defrosting, to the stock pot for extra flavor.

Variations

1. For a gentler tasting broth, omit the turnip, parsnip and garlic. Peel the onion.
2. For a lighter colored broth peel the vegetables.
3. For a Chinese chicken broth, omit everything but the chicken and cold water. Put the chicken in the pot with ⅓ cup rice wine, 2 pieces of ginger the size of a quarter, and 1 cleaned and split green onion. Add the cold water and cook as described.
4. If poached chicken is your primary goal, say for a chicken salad, add the chicken to the boiling water and simmer for 25–30 minutes. Turn off the heat and cool the chicken in the broth. Use the broth as a soup base or for cooking rice or other grains.
5. To use some of the chicken, add breasts, thighs or legs after simmering has begun and remove them after 30 minutes. Use in Spanish Chicken (p. 52), Quick Chicken Curry (p. 51), or Quick Chick (p. 50).

Quick Vegetable Soup

If all else fails, make Quick Vegetable Soup. Instead of water, use liquid from steamed vegetables (it can be stored in the refrigerator). Add chicken or beef stock for a richer soup, or tomato juice for a tangier taste. (Serves 4–6)

Ingredients

3	cups water, broth or juice Salt to taste	⅓	cup fine egg noodles, oatmeal or cornmeal
2	cups grated vegetables (carrots, onions, zucchini, celery)	1	clove thinly chopped garlic
		½	cup finely chopped parsley
2	cups greens, coarsely chopped (celery leaves, parsley, lettuce, spinach)	2	tablespoons butter Salt and freshly ground pepper to taste

Method

Place the water and salt on high heat and bring to a boil. Meanwhile, grate and chop the vegetables. Add to the water, bring to a boil again and boil 5 minutes longer.

Add the noodles or oatmeal and stir well; bring to a boil and simmer another 5 minutes. Add chopped garlic, parsley, butter, and bring to a boil. Add salt and pepper to taste, then serve immediately.

Note: If the soup is too thick add cold milk.

Tuscan Minestrone

Every region of Italy has its own version of minestrone, using pasta, beans and broth. Here is a version from Tuscany, which uses the coarse bread of that region instead of pasta. (Serves 6–8)

Ingredients

8	ounces dried cannellini beans	1½	bunches kale
1	slice prosciutto, about 3 ounces *or*	1	potato
1	ounce salt pork plus 2 ounces boiled ham	1	cup canned tomatoes
1	large red onion	1	small bunch Swiss chard (spinach may be substituted)
1	celery rib	12	large, thick slices Tuscan bread, several days old, or 9–12 large spoons home-made crostini (croutons)
2	large cloves garlic		
1	carrot		Salt and freshly ground pepper
7 or 8	sprigs Italian parsley		
6	tablespoons olive oil	6–8	tablespoons Parmesan cheese, freshly grated
½	small head savoy cabbage		

Method

Soak the dried beans overnight in cold water. To accelerate tenderizing the beans, use 1 or 2 tablespoons flour in the water; this reduces the soaking time about 4 hours. The next day, drain beans and cook them in a large flameproof casserole with 2 quarts of salted water and the prosciutto, or salt pork and ham. As the beans absorb water, keep adding more so that 2 quarts of liquid are maintained at the end of the cooking time. When the beans are tender (about 1 hour) remove casserole from heat and let stand until needed.

Coarsely chop the onion, celery, garlic, carrot and parsley, then sauté them in a stockpot, with the olive oil, for 12–15 minutes. Meanwhile, thinly slice the savoy cabbage; remove the stems from the kale and cut into small pieces; peel the potato and cut it into little squares. When the sautéing vegetables are light brown, add cabbage, kale and potato to the stockpot with the tomatoes. Cover and simmer for 15 minutes, then add cut-up Swiss chard with stems removed. Remove the prosciutto (or salt pork and ham) from the beans. Pass ⅔ of the beans through a food mill into the stockpot. Simmer together for about ½ hour more, until savoy cabbage and kale are almost cooked. Drain the remaining beans, reserving the liquid, and return them to the original casserole. Add the bean liquid to the stockpot, little by little, whenever more liquid is needed until all is used. When the cabbage and kale are ready, add the remaining beans, whole. Taste for salt and pepper, then let cook for 5 minutes more.

If bread is used, put a layer of slices on the bottom of a tureen and pour over two full ladles of soup. Repeat until all the bread is used. Pour the remaining soup on top, cover the tureen and let stand for 20 minutes before serving. Sprinkle 1 tablespoon grated Parmesan over each portion.

If you are using croutons instead of bread slices, place 1½ tablespoons of croutons in each individual soup bowl. Allow the soup to stand for 20 minutes after cooking, then pour over croutons. Sprinkle with grated Parmesan and serve.

Cream of Pumpkin Soup

This soup is originally from Jamaica. Its delicate flavor and color make it a pleasant hot soup for warm weather—a prelude to a salad meal. (Serves 6)

Ingredients

2	tablespoons butter	1	teaspoon brown sugar
¼	cup finely chopped onion	⅛	teaspoon ground mace or nutmeg
1	teaspoon curry powder		
1	tablespoon all-purpose flour	¼	teaspoon salt
3½	cups hot chicken broth	⅛	teaspoon freshly ground black pepper
1	19-ounce (530g) can pumpkin (or fresh pumpkin, acorn, pepper or hubbard squash, cooked and mashed)	1	cup milk, or half-and-half cream (light cream)
			Minced chives or parsley

Method

Heat the butter in a 2-quart pan or larger and sauté onion over medium heat until limp. Stir in curry and flour and cook until bubbly (about 5 minutes). Remove from heat and gradually stir in the hot chicken broth. Add pumpkin, sugar, mace, salt and pepper. Cook, stirring, until the mixture begins to simmer. Stir in the milk and continue heating, but do not boil. Sprinkle a few minced chives or parsley into each bowl when you serve.

Make delicious melba toast, finger-style, as follows: cut each slice of leftover bread into three vertical strips and lay them on a cookie sheet. Let them dry out thoroughly, then toast them golden brown in a slow oven. Serve with soups, salads and dips.

Tomato Soup Portugaise

Portugaise, according to French tradition, means a dish served with tomatoes. In this case, it is a soup made with either fresh or canned tomatoes that is delicate and delicious. I serve it often. It requires no special ingredients, so it can be whipped up quickly when unexpected guests drop in. Try this as the starter course with your favorite macaroni and cheese or cheese soufflé. (Serves 4)

Ingredients

1 tablespoon butter	1 tablespoon tomato paste
2 small onions, sliced	¼ teaspoon sugar
1 clove garlic	1 small bay leaf
2 small potatoes	Salt and freshly ground black pepper to taste
2 fresh tomatoes or 1 14-ounce can (398 mL) tomatoes	Fresh thyme for garnish
3 cups boiling water	

Method

Melt the butter in a saucepan, add the onion and sauté over very low heat for 10 minutes. Add the chopped garlic and continue to sauté for another 5 minutes until the onion is golden but not brown.

Peel the potatoes and cut into cubes. Peel, seed and chop the fresh tomatoes. Add the rest of the ingredients to the pot, cover and simmer for 30 minutes. Discard the bay leaf.

Process the soup in batches in a food processor using the steel knife, or in a blender or food mill. Return to the pot, taste and adjust seasoning. Reheat to serve. Garnish with a sprig of fresh thyme.

When a recipe calls for 1 tablespoon of tomato paste, I am left feeling frustrated about what to do with the remainder.
Simply measure the rest in one tablespoon amounts into each section of your ice cube tray. Freeze. When frozen, remove them and store in a freezer bag. Add the cubes to stews, sauces, beef gravy, chili or soups.

Do all of your recipes call for fresh herbs and if so, how much of the dried herbs may be substituted?
Unless the recipe calls for fresh, the intention is that you use dried herbs. If you have fresh, use twice as much as the amount called for in the recipe. In the case of a specific recipe using fresh herbs, use half the amount of dried herbs for the same effect.

Sweet Potato Soup

A good way to use leftover cooked sweet potatoes. Both the color and flavor are beautiful. (Makes about 6 cups)

Ingredients

1	pound sweet potatoes (about 2 medium ones)	Pinch salt
4	cups chicken broth	Pinch white pepper
½	cup heavy cream	Minced parsley

Method

Bake sweet potatoes until very soft. Peel and cut into 1-inch chunks. Purée sweet potatoes with 1½-2 cups broth in a blender or food processor, adding more broth if too thick. When very smooth, pour into a medium-sized saucepan with remaining broth, cream and seasonings. Heat to serving temperature. Garnish each serving with minced parsley.

Crockpot Potato-Leek Chowder

A hearty chowder for a cold night supper. (Makes 6–8 servings)

Ingredients

6	slices bacon, diced	½	teaspoon dried thyme leaves	
3	large leeks, cleaned well and chopped		Pinch of pepper	
4	medium potatoes, diced	1	cup cooked diced chicken	
1	cup sliced carrots	1	cup milk	
5	cups chicken stock		Parsley	
1	bay leaf		Watercress	

Method

Cook diced bacon until crisp. Drain and set aside. Combine leeks, potatoes, carrots, chicken stock and seasonings in a crockpot. Cover and cook on low heat for 5–6 hours. Half an hour before serving, stir in diced bacon, chicken and milk. To serve, garnish with chopped parsley or sprig of watercress.

Keep scum that forms on soup stock at a minimum by setting the heat low while the stock is cooking. Don't boil soup stock—simmer it.

Beet Borscht

A colorful, tasty soup for hearty eating. Serve with Blue Cheese Toasts (see p. 8). (Makes 6–8 servings)

Ingredients

1½ pounds beets
2 medium onions, chopped
2 stalks celery, chopped
3 tablespoons butter
2 tablespoons flour
6 cups beef broth
1 cup grated carrot
2 tablespoons red wine vinegar
1 bay leaf

Salt to taste
Pinch freshly ground black pepper
½ teaspoon dillweed
¾ cup shredded beet tops
2 tablespoons finely minced fresh parsley
Sour cream or yogurt for garnish

Method

Scrub and peel beets and cut into thin strips 1 inch long. In a large saucepan or Dutch oven sauté onions and celery in butter until vegetables are softened. Stir in flour, mixing well. Add beef broth, beets, carrots, vinegar, bay leaf, salt, pepper and dillweed. Simmer, covered for 30 minutes, until beets are tender. Stir in shredded beet tops and parsley. Simmer 5 minutes more. Garnish each serving with a dollop of sour cream or yogurt.

Dieter's Ratatouille Soup

Ratatouille is a traditional summer salad or vegetable dish made with eggplant, zucchini, tomatoes and olive oil. This soup has the extravagant summer flavor and satisfying taste of ratatouille without the oil. Forty-two calories for one serving! This soup tastes best if the flavors are allowed to blend for a day or two. (One serving)

Ingredients

2 tablespoons chopped onion
3 tablespoons cubed green or red pepper
½ cup or more cubed zucchini
½ cup or more cubed eggplant
¼ teaspoon hot pepper, minced, or pinch dried hot peppers

1 tablespoon minced parsley
¼ teaspoon garlic salt
Pinch dried oregano
Pinch freshly ground pepper
1 6-ounce (177mL) can or ¾ cup vegetable juice

Method

Heat a fat-free pan (e.g., Silverstone or T-Fal) and add the onion, stirring to soften for about 1–2 minutes. Add pepper and stir. Add zucchini, eggplant and hot pepper, cover and simmer over low heat for 4–5 minutes. Add parsley and seasonings; stir to blend. Mix in vegetable juice, then pour into a container and cover. Store in the refrigerator. When ready to serve garnish with a dollop of yogurt or a lemon slice.

Cold Cucumber and Spinach Soup

A jar of this thick green soup in the refrigerator during the hot summer months makes meal planning simpler. A cool bowlful, garnished with yogurt or sour cream, a sprinkling of fresh dill and some crisp bits of scallion is a welcome invitation to enjoyable dining. Follow this with a hearty salad or barbecued chicken. (Makes 7 cups or enough for 14 servings)

Ingredients

1¾	cups rich chicken broth or 1 10-ounce can plus ½ cup water	2	green onions—bulbs about ½ inch in diameter
7½	cups fresh cucumber chunks, washed and seeded	1	teaspoon fresh dillweed
			Pinch dried tarragon
3½	cups well-packed spinach leaves, washed, with stems removed	3	green peppercorns
		½-1	teaspoon salt

Garnish

Yogurt or sour cream   Green onion
Fresh dillweed

Method

Bring the broth to the boil and add cucumber. Simmer for 5 minutes. Add the balance of the ingredients, making sure to layer the spinach above the cucumber so that it will steam while the cucumber softens. Simmer for another 5 minutes or until the spinach is limp. Cool slightly. Whirl in two batches in a food processor or blender until smooth, or use a hand food mill to purée. Store in a covered container in the refrigerator.

To serve

Chill the serving bowls. Into each ladle ½ cup soup purée and add ⅓ cup yogurt, either in a swirl or a dollop. Garnish with fresh dillweed and a sprinkling of green onion slices.

Iced Sorrel Soup

Sorrel has become very popular lately and it is at its best in this simple soup. It loses flavor when dried so try to buy fresh sorrel at the markets in summer. If you grow your own and you wish to store it, I suggest you wash, chop the leaves and soften them in butter for a few minutes, then freeze in small quantities for later use. Sorrel combines well with chicken stock as a cream soup or as a chiffonade for chicken or fish sauté. (Serves 4)

Ingredients

1	cup sorrel leaves, packed	3	tablespoons chopped fresh dill
1	tablespoon butter		Salt
3	cups plain yogurt		Freshly ground black pepper
1	medium cucumber, seeded		

Method

Wash the sorrel and remove the heavy stem. Soften briefly in butter, then place in blender jar or food processor. Taste the yogurt. If it is very sharp, you may want to add a bit of sugar. Wash the cucumber. If the peel is thin, leave it on. Otherwise, peel and seed it and add, along with dill and ¼ cup yogurt to the sorrel. Process or blend until fine. Pour into a container and blend with remaining yogurt. Taste and adjust seasoning with salt and pepper as needed. Refrigerate and serve in chilled bowls, garnished with sprigs of fresh dill.

Chilly Tomato Bisque

An inviting summertime soup using fresh tomatoes that adds color to the table and is quick to make. Is is also low in calories. (Makes 4 cups)

Ingredients

1½	cups vegetable juice	½	teaspoon salt
1	cup plain yogurt		Sprinkling of pepper
4	medium tomatoes, peeled, seeded and chopped (see p. 97)		Parsley, mint as garnish
1	tablespoon fresh basil leaves or 1 teaspoon dried basil		

Method

Combine all ingredients in a blender or food processor jar and process until smooth. Pour into a large jar and refrigerate for several hours to blend the flavors. Serve well chilled. Garnish with chopped parsley or chopped fresh mint.

BEEF, PORK, VEAL, LAMB
AND ORGAN MEATS

BEEF
Spicy Pot Roast 26
Burger Stroganoff 26
Curried Beef 27
Pasta Meat Sauce 28
Sweet and Sour Beef Stew 29
Sweet Potato Beef Pie 29

PORK
Pork and Beer Chili 30
Red and Orange Spareribs 31
Stuffed Acorn Squash 32

VEAL
Veal Shanks
with Creole Sauce 32
Lavinia's Veal Roast 34

LAMB
Lamb Sauce for Pasta 35
Lamb Fricassee 36

ORGAN MEATS
Stir-fried Liver with Onions 36
Calf's Liver with Marsala Wine 38
Sautéed Chicken Livers with Port Wine 38
Chicken Livers with Vegetables 39
Kidneys in Sherry Sauce 40
Kidneys and Mushroom Casserole 41

Spicy Pot Roast

For this recipe I like using a crockpot because it looks after itself and there are many times when the thought of dinner simmering unattended in the kitchen is reassuring to a busy person. This dependable recipe uses economical cuts of beef and tastes delicious. Serve with mashed potatoes and buttered carrots, or baked potato and French green beans. (Serves 6–8)

Ingredients

5	pounds blade, cross-rib, short-rib or shoulder roast	1	cup tomato juice if using crockpot or 2 cups otherwise
2	tablespoons shortening	1	cup chopped onion
½	teaspoon dried thyme	1	bay leaf
2	tablespoons sugar	1½	teaspoons salt
1	tablespoon vinegar		Pinch of freshly ground black pepper
1	clove garlic, minced, or ½ teaspoon garlic salt		

Method

Brown meat on all sides in shortening. Combine remaining ingredients and pour over meat. Cover and simmer 3–3½ hours until tender. Strain gravy and thicken with flour.

Burger Stroganoff

A quick skillet dish, this ground beef stroganoff can be prepared at the last minute. If the beef is fatty, don't add the vegetable oil at all: just let it sauté in the beef drippings. If you are worried about extra fat in your diet try to drain it off. Serve with green peas or beans. (Serves 6)

Ingredients

2	pounds lean ground beef	3	tablespoons tomato paste
2	tablespoons vegetable oil (if required)	1–3	tablespoons spicy brown or Dijon mustard (optional)
1	large Spanish onion, peeled and rather coarsely chopped	1	tablespoon anchovy paste (optional)
1	large clove garlic, peeled and minced	⅛	teaspoon freshly ground black pepper
1	pound mushrooms, wiped clean, trimmed of coarse stem ends and sliced thin		Salt to taste
3	large, very ripe tomatoes, peeled, cored and chopped, include juice (see p. 97)	⅓–¾	cup sour cream, at room temperature

Method

In a large heavy skillet, over moderately high heat, brown the beef lightly in the vegetable oil (if needed). Break up large clumps. Add the onion, garlic and mushrooms and stir-fry along with the beef for about 10 minutes, or until vegetables are limp and golden. Stir in the tomatoes and their juice, tomato paste, the mustard and/or anchovy paste (if using) and the pepper. Reduce the heat and simmer, covered, for 30 minutes, then cover and simmer for 20–25 minutes longer, stirring often, until the mixture has reduced to a sauce-like consistency. Taste for salt and season as needed.

Smooth in the sour cream (do not allow to boil or the cream may curdle) then serve over buttered noodles or fluffy boiled rice.

Curried Beef

An easy curry to prepare for a busy day. Serve over cooked rice. (Makes 4–6 servings)

Ingredients

1½ pounds stewing beef, cut into 1-inch cubes
1 medium onion, chopped
1 clove garlic, minced
½ pound sliced mushrooms
1 5½-ounce (156 mL) can tomato paste

1 cup beef stock
1-2 teaspoons curry powder

2 tablespoons flour (optional)
½ cup water (optional)

Method

Combine all ingredients in a slow cooker, such as a crockpot, cover and cook on low heat for 6 hours. If using the oven, place ingredients in a covered casserole and bake at 300°F for 3 hours or until tender.

Before serving, spoon off excess fat from sauce, if necessary. Sauce may be thickened, if desired. Combine 2 tablespoons flour with ½ cup water, until smooth. Stir into beef mixture. Cover and cook 15 minutes longer.

To improve the texture of hamburgers, as well as their shape, add a few drops of water to the meat, then shape meat into patties and let them stand 10 minutes or more before cooking.

Pasta Meat Sauce

Meat sauces for pasta differ throughout Italy. Some use garlic, others do not. Some use beef and wine, still others do not. This one is a typical northern sauce and comes from the kitchen of Giuliano Bugialli in Florence. It is best served with a hearty pasta—spaghetti, penne or small shells, and with a robust Chianti red wine. (Makes 2–2½ cups)

Ingredients

1	ounce dried porcini mushrooms (or a small package)	½	pound beef sirloin, in one piece
1	cup lukewarm water	½	cup dry red wine
1	carrot		Salt and freshly ground black pepper to taste
1	celery rib		
1	medium-sized red onion	1	16-ounce (454 g) can Italian plum tomatoes
6–7	sprigs Italian parsley		
1	clove garlic	1	tablespoon tomato paste
	Small piece of lemon peel	2	cups hot meat or chicken broth
¼	cup olive oil		

Method

Soak the mushrooms in lukewarm water for 25–30 minutes. Thinly chop the carrot, celery, onion, parsley, garlic and lemon peel, then place in a flameproof casserole (preferably earthenware) with the olive oil. Sauté very gently until golden brown (about 15–20 minutes). With scissors, snip the meat into tiny pieces and add to the contents of the casserole. Sauté the meat pieces for 12–15 minutes, then add the wine and cook until it evaporates (15–20 minutes). Taste for salt and pepper, then add the tomatoes and tomato paste and let cook very slowly for 20–25 minutes.

Drain the soaked mushrooms through two layers of paper towelling to remove any grit. Reserve the soaking liquid. Remove mushrooms and chop coarsely. Add the mushrooms to the sauce and simmer very slowly for at least 1½ hours, adding hot broth and the water in which mushrooms have been soaked as liquid is needed, until all the broth and mushroom water have been added. (The sauce should be of medium thickness, neither too liquid nor too dense).

If the recipe calls for herbs and spices that don't dissolve—such as bay leaves, whole cloves, garlic buds—tuck them into a metal teaball. With the teaball chain hooked over the side of the pan, it's easy to remove seasonings after cooking, or before, if the flavors threaten to become too strong.

Sweet and Sour Beef Stew

Here's a hearty stew whose unusual sauce makes it extraordinary. It freezes well and reheats equally well. Serve with crusty bread, boiled potatoes, Brussels sprouts and a gelatin dessert. (Serves 6–8)

Ingredients

3	tablespoons flour	½	cup molasses
½	teaspoon salt	⅓	cup red wine vinegar
½	teaspoon celery salt	2	medium onions, sliced
½	teaspoon ginger	6	carrots
2	pounds stewing beef (cubed)	1	cup raw, cleaned cranberries
3	teaspoons oil	½	cup raisins
1	28-ounce (796 mL) can tomatoes		

Method

Combine flour and seasoning; coat beef cubes with mixture and brown in hot oil in Dutch oven. Stir in tomatoes, molasses, vinegar and onions; cover and simmer for 2 hours. Add remaining ingredients and cook until tender, about 15 minutes.

Sweet Potato Beef Pie

An unusual way to serve ground beef. Team it with a green salad for an easy appetizing meal. (Serves 6)

Ingredients

1	pound ground beef		Pinch of thyme
1	medium onion, chopped	2	tablespoons flour
1	stalk celery, chopped	1	teaspoon Worcestershire sauce
1	tomato, peeled, seeded and chopped (see p. 97)	1	cup beef broth
	Pinch of salt	2	cups peeled and diced sweet potatoes (about 1 medium one)
	Pinch of freshly ground black pepper	1	baked 9-inch pastry shell

Method

Preheat oven to 400°F. In a large skillet, crumble ground beef and cook until lightly browned. Drain off excess fat. Stir in onion and celery and soften. Add tomato, salt, pepper and thyme. Sprinkle with flour and mix well. Add Worcestershire sauce, broth and potatoes. Cover and simmer for 15 minutes. Turn into baked pastry shell, cover loosely with foil and bake for 20–25 minutes.

Pork and Beer Chili

Everyone feels that their chili recipe is the best; I am no exception. In my opinion, this is the best chili I've made.

The combination of pork, raisins, cumin and chili renders this simple dish superb. It's a good budget stretcher, too. Use dried beans if there's time and add more beans to the amount required if you're having a crowd. Serve with a tossed green salad spiked with red onion, cucumber and radishes, a brown rice casserole, pumpernickel bread and ginger beer! (Serves 8–10 amply)

Ingredients

1	large onion, chopped		1	teaspoon dry mustard
1 or 2	cloves garlic, chopped thinly		2	teaspoons salt
1¼	pounds pork, very lean, ground		1	teaspoon cumin
3	tablespoons light vegetable oil			Freshly ground black pepper
1	cup beer		2	cans (398 mL each) kidney beans and liquid
1	can (540 mL) tomatoes		½	cup light raisins
2	tablespoons flour			
1½	tablespoons chili powder			

Method

Heat the oil in a heavy Dutch oven and add onion and garlic. Sweat over medium heat, stirring, until golden—about 10 minutes. Move aside and add the pork. (I like to buy pork shoulder, remove the visible fat and grind it in the food processor.) Cook the pork until it is no longer pink, stirring to break up the lumps.

Add the beer, tomatoes, flour and seasonings. Stir until blended. Bring to a boil, reduce to simmer, cover and simmer for an hour, stirring occasionally. Taste. Add salt, pepper and other seasonings as necessary. Remove the cover, add beans with their liquid and raisins. Simmer for another 10 minutes. Serve hot. This chili tastes even better reheated.

Drain fruit or kidney beans for salad the easy way—puncture the top of the can before opening it and invert the can in a container to store the liquid. When liquid has been drained, open the can and remove the contents.

Red and Orange Spareribs

This delicious sweet and tart sparerib casserole tastes lovely with fluffy mashed potatoes and green slivered beans. Prepare the ribs in a clay baker, or use a microwave oven if you have one. (Serves 6)

Ingredients

3	pounds lean back spareribs, trimmed of excess fat and cut into six pieces	1/2	cup cranberries, washed and dried
1	clove garlic, minced	1	lemon, washed and sliced thinly
1	onion, sliced		
1	tablespoon brown sugar	1 1/2	tablespoons Worcestershire sauce
1/2	teaspoon ginger	1	tablespoon soya sauce
1/2	teaspoon cinnamon	1/2	cup beef or chicken broth or the pork simmering liquid
1	teaspoon salt		
1/2	cup dried apricots		

Method

To reduce the fat from the ribs parboil them in 1 cup of water. Remove liquid to the refrigerator. The fat will congeal on the top and the broth beneath may be used for this recipe.

Soak the top and bottom of the clay baker in water for about 15 minutes to absorb moisture. Lay the spareribs on the bottom, sprinkle with garlic, onion and a mixture of the dry ingredients. Add fruits and bake at 325°F for 1 1/2 hours, turning 4 times throughout the baking time.

Note: If you have a microwave cook the spareribs at full power for 15 minutes then continue cooking them in the regular oven. Simply drain the liquid and chill it to remove the fat. Or continue in the microwave after the first 15 minutes with the power reduced to half for about 1 hour.

I would like to use your recipes for my work in a group home but I need to make servings for 24. Are there any problems doing this?

Not really. When you bake, of course, it is better to make several batches of the same recipe. When you cook, doubling is simple. You should never double the seasonings, however. Instead, use only the original amount, and taste before adding more.

Stuffed Acorn Squash

Cooking for one or two? This simple, inexpensive main dish uses fall vegetables and ground pork. Serve with garlic spinach, a tomato salad and strawberry ice. (Serves 2)

Ingredients

1	acorn squash	2	tablespoons water
1/3	cup hot water	1/4	teaspoon dry mustard
1/4	cup broken narrow noodles		Salt and freshly ground black
1/4	pound ground pork		pepper to taste
1 1/2	teaspoons flour		Butter

Method

Slice squash in half and remove seeds. Lay squash, sliced side down, in baking dish and add hot water. Bake the squash in a moderately hot oven, 375°F, for approximately 30 minutes, or until the squash is tender.

Cook broken noodles in boiling salted water until they are just tender and drain well. Brown pork in a frying pan. Drain off excess fat. Sprinkle the pork with flour, stir well and add water. Heat the mixture to boiling, then combine the meat with the noodles. Combine dry mustard with salt and pepper and add to mixture. Brush the cavities of the cooked squash with just enough butter to coat. Fill the squash with the meat and noodle mixture and bake at 375°F for 15–20 minutes.

Veal Shanks with Creole Sauce

A stew prepared with bony cuts of meat is always more succulent than one without bones because of the extra gelatin and flavor they impart. Bony meats require long, slow cooking to allow them to yield their richness, so I always prepare this dish on a weekend and let it simmer in the oven for a long time. Then it spends a day or so in the refrigerator. When it's needed, I put it back into a clay pot for another hour in the oven. Served with cooked noodles and a tossed salad, it can only be described as delicious. (Serves 4)

Ingredients

4	pounds veal shanks cut into 2-inch pieces	2	large stalks of celery with the leaves, sliced
1/2	cup flour seasoned with salt and pepper	1	large green or red pepper, halved, seeded and sliced
1/4	cup light vegetable oil	2	cloves garlic, peeled
4	medium onions, sliced		

1 large can (540 mL) tomatoes	Tabasco sauce
1½ cups beef bouillon	Salt and freshly ground black pepper to taste
2 tablespoons vinegar	
2 tablespoons honey	
1 bay leaf	

Method

Slit the membranes of each shank and tie with string. If the shanks are not slit they will bend and be unattractive. Place the seasoned flour in a plastic bag and toss the shanks to coat them with the mixture. Heat the oil in a large, heavy saucepan and brown the shanks well. Remove them with a slotted spoon to a claybaker or casserole. Add the vegetables and garlic to the pan and, stirring often, allow them to soften. When they are golden, remove them to the casserole with the shanks. Add the tomatoes and bouillon to the pan and heat, stirring to remove all of the bits of meat and vegetables from the pan. Pour this mixture over the meat in the casserole. Add the bay leaf, vinegar, honey and a few drops of Tabasco. Cover and place in the oven. Cook at 350°F for about 3 hours.

Test the meat with a fork to see that it is tender. Remove the meat into a bowl with a slotted spoon. Remove half of the sauce along with the vegetables to a blender, food processor or food mill and purée. Pour into another bowl with the remaining vegetable sauce, cover and refrigerate. The fat will rise to the top of the sauce and harden. It should be discarded before the sauce is reheated. When ready to serve, put the meat and sauce together in a clay pot or casserole and heat in the oven. Taste and add seasonings, if necessary.

Hints

This may all be prepared in a covered heavy pan and simmered gently on top of the stove.

If there are no shanks, use veal shoulder and have the butcher give you other bones—a knuckle would be superb.

There will be extra sauce—freeze it. Reheat and pour it over a boiled tongue or plain meat loaf.

Lavinia's Veal Roast

Lavinia, *la mia buona cuoca* has been cooking wonderful meals for some 60 years. It's all but impossible to capture accurately her technique or recipes, although I have tried. We sat together for some time trying to duplicate her simple but succulent veal roast. When veal prices are high, I substitute pork for veal with superb results. (Serves 4 to 6)

Ingredients

2	pounds lean roast of veal—leg, shoulder, or rack, either rolled or unrolled	1	stalk fresh sage or 1 table-spoon dried
	Salt	3	tablespoons butter, cut into small chunks
	White pepper	2	cups milk or broth for basting, approximately (Lavinia uses warm milk)
	Rind of 1 lemon		
2	stalks fresh rosemary or 2 tablespoons dried		

Method

Sprinkle the roast with salt and white pepper and liberally sprinkle with rosemary and sage. Arrange the butter pieces on the roast and sprinkle the lemon rind around it. Place in a very hot 450°F oven to brown and keep turning it over so that it browns evenly. The roast may be browned also on top of the stove.

When the meat has reached the desired color, reduce the heat to 325°F and cover. Baste continually! Add a tablespoon of milk or broth as required to prevent the pan from drying out. Roast until a meat thermometer registers 170°F or for 20 minutes per pound in the oven. A meat thermometer is essential for top-of-the-stove cooking as it takes longer to cook; how much longer depends on the heat of your element.

Note: This roast can dry out, if left unbasted.

Option: I think this meat tastes even better if a couple of chopped onions are added to the pan along with the lemon rind. Also, some parboiled potatoes and small onions can be added about ½ hour before serving.

To Reheat: Prepare this roast early in the day and remove to a board. Slice and place in a shallow casserole surrounded by the vegetables. Deglaze the pan with boiling water or stock. Refrigerate the pan juices until the fat hardens on top. Remove the fat. Heat the juices, pour over the roast, cover lightly and reheat in a 325°F oven for about 20 minutes. Lavinia insists that this dish be served at room temperature. You're on your own there.

Lamb Sauce for Pasta

Giuliano Bugialli captivated his students with this delicious sauce in his kitchen in Florence, Italy. It was certainly the hit of the week. (Serves 6)

Ingredients

12 ounces lamb shoulder meat	¾ cup dry white wine
1 scant tablespoon salt	1 cup canned Italian plum tomatoes
½ teaspoon freshly ground black pepper	2 green peppers, seeded and cut into long strips
6 tablespoons olive oil	
2 medium-sized garlic cloves	
2 bay leaves	

Method

With scissors snip lamb meat off the bone into small pieces about ½-inch square. Place lamb pieces in small bowl, add salt and pepper and mix thoroughly with a wooden spoon. Pour olive oil into a medium-sized saucepan, preferably earthenware or enamel, and place pan over moderate heat. When oil is warm, add peeled, whole garlic cloves and bay leaves. Sauté gently until a very light golden-brown color is reached, then add the lamb, raise the heat and sauté for about 15 minutes, mixing every so often with the wooden spoon.

Add wine, reduce heat, cover pan with lid and let wine evaporate for about 15 minutes. Then add tomatoes and sauté without lid for 10 minutes more. Mix in peppers, cover pan again and let simmer for 1 hour, stirring every so often. If sauce gets too thick, add ¼ cup hot broth or water. Reheat and serve with noodles or spaghetti.

Strain pasta, place on serving dish and pour sauce over. Serve immediately. Do not add cheese.

Lamb Fricassee

A leg of lamb for a family of two seems, at first, ridiculous. If you slice chops off the sirloin end, stew bits from the underside and cube lamb for this fricassee from the top, there'll be enough for roast leg of lamb and soup from the bones. Have a sharp knife handy and do the butchering yourself. This dish is delicious served with carrots or green beans. (Serves 2)

Ingredients

1	large onion, chopped	¾	cup water
1	tablespoon light vegetable oil	1	egg yolk
1	pound lamb cubes, about 1½ inches		Juice from ½ large lemon
1	teaspoon dried marjoram	1	tablespoon water
1	teaspoon dried basil	1	tablespoon chopped parsley
1	small clove garlic, chopped (optional)		

Method

Heat oil in a large, heavy saucepan and soften onion. Add the lamb and allow it to brown on each side. Add the herbs and garlic, if desired, as the lamb cooks. Add the water, cover and bring to the boil. Reduce the heat and let the lamb simmer for one hour, covered. Remove the meat to a warm serving platter. Skim off the fat from the top of the gravy. Taste the gravy and add salt, if necessary. Lightly beat the egg yolk with the lemon juice and another 1 tablespoon water and add to the gravy, whisking over low heat until it thickens. Then pour over lamb. Sprinkle with chopped parsley and serve.

Stir-Fried Liver with Onions

A wok isn't needed for stir-frying, but if you have one, use it. Otherwise, find a large-bottomed frypan—large enough to hold the liver in a single layer for quick cooking. Vary the recipe, too. If there are no green onions, use frozen green beans or broccoli; add tiny corn cobs or pea pods. Serve hot with steamed rice, sweet and sour carrots and a salad of asparagus or cucumber. (Serves 4)

Ingredients

¾	pound thinly sliced baby beef or calf's liver

Marinade

½ teaspoon salt
½ teaspoon freshly ground black pepper

2 teaspoons cornstarch
2 teaspoons pale, dry sherry
2 teaspoons sesame oil

Vegetables

6 green onions, cut into 2-inch pieces
1 cup water chestnuts, rinsed in boiling water and thinly sliced
½ cup dried tree ears (mushrooms) softened in 1 cup boiling water

Pea pods, broccoli, green beans, canned corn cobs (optional)

Sauce

2 tablespoons soya sauce
1 teaspoon sugar
1 tablespoon rice wine vinegar
1 tablespoon pale, dry sherry
1 tablespoon cornstarch

1 cup water drained from the soaking mushrooms or chicken stock

7 tablespoons vegetable oil
2 slices ginger, finely chopped

Method

Rinse the liver, pat dry and slice into 2-inch pieces (the same as the green onions). Combine marinade ingredients in a large bowl, slice the vegetables, and mix sauce ingredients together in a measuring cup. Place the liver slices in a bowl with the marinade, cover and set aside for at least ½ hour.

When ready to cook and serve, heat 4 tablespoons oil in the wok until a drop of water skitters over the surface. Add liver and marinade, stir-fry rapidly for 1 minute and remove to a plate. (The liver will absorb marinade.) Heat remaining 3 tablespoons oil. Add ginger and press against the sides. Add vegetables and stir-fry for 1 minute. Return liver to the wok, stir the sauce and add. Simmer and stir until thickened—about 12 minutes longer.

Calf's Liver with Marsala Wine

Fresh liver arrives in the meat markets in Rome each Wednesday morning and by noon it is gone. Italians have a fondness for liver that is reflected in the care and delicacy with which it is served in restaurants and homes. (Serves 4)

Ingredients

1	pound calf's liver, sliced thinly and evenly	1	teaspoon salt
2	tablespoons lemon juice	2	tablespoons butter
1/3	cup flour	2	tablespoons light vegetable oil
1/4	teaspoon white pepper, freshly ground, if possible	3	tablespoons Marsala or sweet sherry

Method

Wipe the liver dry, removing any membranes. Rub the surface with the lemon juice. Set aside for 15 minutes. Toss the liver in a plastic bag containing the flour, salt and pepper. Heat the butter and oil in a sauté pan until a drop of flour sizzles. Maintain the heat and drop in the liver, cooking quickly for a minute on each side. The liver will still have a faint pink tinge. Add the wine, reduce heat and baste the liver as it continues cooking, for another few moments only.

Sautéed Chicken Livers with Port Wine

Port wine combines with everything including chicken livers. Together they make a regal dish. Try this with a white rice pilaf and steamed celery and tomatoes. (Serves 6)

Ingredients

Liver

1	pound chicken livers Flour, salt and freshly ground black pepper for dredging	2	tablespoons oil or butter

Sauce

1	cup port wine Juice of 1 orange	1	tablespoon butter
1	teaspoon chicken-flavored crystals or 1 small chicken cube	1/3	cup milk or cream

Method

Prepare the sauce by combining the juice of the orange and port wine in a saucepan and boiling for 10 minutes or until the volume is reduced by half. Add the chicken cube and butter and continue to cook for another 5 minutes. Stir the milk well into the mixture. Set aside while preparing the liver.

Remove any bits of fat or gristle from the livers, cut each in half and wash. Drop into a plastic bag with the flour mixture and toss to coat. Brown liver pieces in a large sauté pan with oil or butter; turn gently, using tongs. They are ready when there is no longer any pink showing. Place livers on a warmed platter heaped with rice or on individual serving plates and pour the hot sauce over top.

Chicken Livers with Vegetables

Once you plan to go on a diet, make a batch of chicken stock and keep it handy in serving-size packages. It is indispensable, for it can replace oil and butter. In this recipe the livers and vegetables are sautéed in broth instead of butter. That is a saving of 70–100 calories, and few would notice the difference in taste. Serve with a side salad of lettuce, mixed with lemon, tomato or yogurt dressing. Only 70 calories in each serving. (1 Serving)

Ingredients

1   tablespoon chicken broth
½   medium onion, cut in quarters
½   green pepper, cut in eighths
¼   pound chicken livers, cleaned and halved

2   teaspoons Worcestershire sauce
½   tomato, seeded and cut into quarters

Note: Pieces of liver and pieces of vegetable should be the same size and shape, if possible

Method

Heat a sauté or frying pan large enough to hold the vegetables and livers. Add broth. Add onion and cook lightly until soft—about 3–4 minutes. Add pepper, livers and Worcestershire sauce and sauté lightly, stirring until the livers have turned brown. Cover and simmer for 3–4 minutes. Add tomatoes and heat for about 2 minutes. Remove the livers and vegetables to a warming plate, then reduce gravy by boiling it until there are only 2 tablespoons left. Pour over livers and serve.

Kidneys in Sherry Sauce

Kidneys are very nutritious and taste delightful when cooked carefully. Beef and pork kidneys are quite large and require pre-soaking in salted, acidulous water; veal and lamb kidneys are smaller and tender enough to be sautéed without any pre-soaking. You'll need 2–3 lamb or 1 veal kidney per serving. When preparing the smaller kidneys, sauté them quickly over moderate heat, then slice and keep them on a warmed platter while the sauce is prepared. Cooking over a high heat toughens them.

This simple, quick recipe may be prepared in a chafing dish right at the table. Serve with steaming tomato-and-green-pepper rice. A fresh vegetable such as carrots or broccoli is excellent with these kidneys. (Serves 6)

Ingredients

2	tablespoons light vegetable oil	1	tablespoon flour
16	lamb or 6 veal kidneys, cleaned	½	cup chicken stock
1	onion, chopped		Pinch of salt
2	cloves garlic, crushed		Pinch freshly ground black pepper
½	cup dry sherry		
2	tablespoons butter		

Method

Heat the oil in a medium-sized frypan. When hot, add the whole kidneys and stir-fry for 2–3 minutes. They should remain pink in the centre. *Note:* If using veal kidneys, they should be sautéed for 10 minutes. Remove the kidneys from the pan, slice into serving-size pieces, place on a heated platter and cover to keep warm.

Add onion and garlic and sauté until golden yellow. Remove to platter. Add sherry to deglaze the pan and set aside. In the same pan, melt the butter and stir in flour to make a roux. Stir for a minute or two. Gradually add the stock and sherry to the roux and cook for 5 minutes or more to make a sauce. Taste and season with salt and pepper if necessary. Add the onion, garlic and kidneys to the sauce and heat.

Kidneys and Mushroom Casserole

Port wine adds a full, sweet flavor to kidneys. This casserole is special and simple. Use it for guests or as a plain dinner after work. Dieters should omit the oil and the browning step. Serve with steamed rice, cabbage and fruit salad. Ice cream or sherbet and cookies make a good, light dessert. (Serves 2)

Ingredients

½	pound beef kidney	1	tablespoon light vegetable oil
2	tablespoons all-purpose flour	¼	cup port wine
1	teaspoon salt	1	tablespoon Dijon mustard
	Pinch freshly ground black pepper	¼	pound large mushrooms, whole

Method

Slice the kidney into ¼-inch slices and, using kitchen scissors, remove the fatty membrane that runs throughout. Soak the kidney slices in water to which you have added a drop of vinegar and salt. Leave them to soak for no less than 1 hour but as long as all day.

When you are ready to prepare the kidneys, dry them well and coat with the flour mixed with salt and pepper. Heat the oil in a casserole and add the kidneys, stirring to brown them lightly. Let them cook very gently for about 5 minutes, turning them around so that they cook on all sides. Add the port wine and mustard, cover and place in a 300°F oven for 1 hour. Add the mushrooms and continue baking another ½ hour. Serve hot.

POULTRY

Hunter's-Style Chicken

Star anise and fennel give this tomato and chicken combination its unique taste. If you have neither in the house, it would be worthwhile to stop and pick some up at a health food or speciality store. Low in calories and fat but flavorful enough for guests, Hunter's-Style Chicken is different and exciting. Make it in quantity for a buffet supper. Serve with fresh steamed cauliflower or broccoli, buttered noodles, and a light salad, followed by fruit dipped in chocolate or a simple apple tart. (Serves 6)

Ingredients

3½ pounds chicken pieces   Salt, pepper

Sauce

2   19-ounce (540 mL) cans Italian plum tomatoes
2   tablespoons olive oil
½   cup dry white wine
½   cup chopped onion
2   garlic cloves, chopped
1   small piece orange rind, about 1 inch × 1½ inches

1   bay leaf
½   teaspoon fennel seeds
1   star anise
½   teaspoon coriander
¼   teaspoon cinnamon

Garnish
Black olives

Method

Preheat oven to 350°F. Drain tomatoes (reserve the juice) and crush the pulp with your hands into a small saucepan. Add the remaining sauce ingredients, cover and simmer for 30 minutes. Then remove the bay leaf, anise and orange peel.

Meanwhile arrange the chicken pieces in a baking dish and sprinkle with salt and pepper. Pour the sauce over the chicken, making certain that all pieces are coated. Cover the dish with a lid or aluminum foil and bake for about 1½ hours or until the chicken is tender. (If the sauce seems a little dry during the baking, add some of the reserved tomato juice.) Garnish the top of the baked chicken with black olives.

Chicken Breasts Florentine

When your long lost cousin arrives in town for one night and you'd like to entertain at dinner, choose this. Simple, quick to prepare, with ingredients that are always in season, you can rush in and have an elegant dinner on the table in about an hour. And it's been child-tested—they love it! Serve with sliced tomato vinaigrette topped with green onion, boiled and buttered new potatoes and tender carrots. (Serves 4)

Ingredients

Chicken Mixture

1–1½	pounds boneless chicken breasts	¼	cup dry white wine (about #1 on the liquor board listing)
2	teaspoons butter		
1	small shallot, or ½ a small onion, chopped	½	cup chicken broth

Spinach Mixture

1 or 2	packages of frozen chopped spinach (have the larger amount for spinach lovers) *or*	1	tablespoon melted butter
		1	tablespoon fresh dill, minced or ½ tablespoon dried dill weed or seed
1	4-cup (1 litre) package fresh spinach, washed, cooked and chopped		Pinch each of salt, freshly ground black pepper and nutmeg

Sauce

1	tablespoon butter	½	cup milk (for low-calorie diet use skim milk)
1	tablespoon flour		
	Liquid reserved from the chicken	1	egg yolk

Topping

3	tablespoons Parmesan cheese, freshly grated

Method

For best results assemble just before serving. Prepare the spinach mixture and arrange in a casserole. Prepare the chicken breasts and place over the spinach. Prepare the sauce, cover and keep warm. Grate the cheese, and set aside.

Spinach

Cook frozen spinach according to package instructions. If using fresh spinach, wash well and remove tough stems. Steam in the water adhering to the leaves. Drain, dry with paper towel and squeeze all water out. Toss with butter, dill, salt, pepper and nutmeg.

Chicken
Soften the shallots, or onion, in the butter until just golden brown and soft. Pour wine and broth over, cover and bring to boil. Add chicken and simmer breasts for 15 minutes, or until they are done (your finger will leave a mark when pressed). Remove the breasts to a covered casserole and keep warm. Pour the liquid into a pitcher.

Sauce
Heat the butter, add the flour and stir until well blended. Add the chicken liquid, stirring constantly until it is cooked. Add the milk, continue to cook for about 3 minutes, then remove from heat and stir in the egg yolk. Return to a low heat and cook about 2 minutes. Reserve, covered.

To Assemble
About 30 minutes before serving preheat broiler. Pour the sauce over the spinach and chicken. Sprinkle with the grated cheese and place under the broiler until the cheese is crusty and faintly golden brown. (If spinach, chicken and sauce have cooled before broiling, place them, covered, in a 325°F oven for 30 minutes, then broil.)

Crispy Broiled Chicken Breast
Here is a quick, broiled chicken recipe that can be made for one or several servings. This simple dish requires little preparation and blends well with a quick salad or steamed green vegetable. If you're making it for just one or two, use a toaster oven instead of the broiler. The chicken could also be done on the barbecue. (Serves 1 or more)

Ingredients

Each serving requires

½	chicken breast	2	teaspoons Dijon mustard
2	teaspoons Pommery mustard	½	teaspoon Worcestershire sauce

Method

Leave the rib bones attached to the breast. Place under the broiler about 1½ inches from the element. Broil the breast for 1 minute, or until you see the fat ooze from the skin. Cover well with mustards and Worcestershire sauce and return to the broiler. Broil until almost black and very crisp. If the breasts are thick and need more cooking time (test with your finger—the meat should spring back when pressed in the thickest section) turn on the oven to 350°F and continue cooking 3–4 minutes longer.

Hint
Dieters should remove the skin after the first broiling period to reduce calories.

Sautéed Chicken with Vinegar

Here is a simple way to prepare fried chicken with a delicious sauce. Serve with fresh asparagus and new potatoes with parsley for a springtime dinner. (Serves 4)

Ingredients

½ cup butter, clarified (see below)

1 chicken cut into serving pieces
Salt and freshly ground black pepper

3 tablespoons minced shallots (2 or 3)

½ cup red wine

½ cup red wine vinegar

3 tablespoons soft butter cut into pieces

1 tablespoon rosemary

Method

Heat the butter in a skillet just large enough to hold the chicken pieces comfortably. Salt and pepper the chicken and sauté over high heat for 5 minutes, browning on all sides. Cover the skillet and reduce the temperature to low. Continue cooking, covered, for 20 minutes, turning the chicken once after 10 minutes. Remove chicken to a heated plate and keep warm in a 200°F oven.

Pour off all but 1 tablespoon of fat from the pan and quickly sauté the shallots without letting them brown. Pour the wine and vinegar into the skillet and stir with a wooden spoon until all the brown bits are loosened. Boil until the liquid is reduced by half. Remove the skillet from the heat and whisk in the 3 tablespoons of butter and rosemary. Pour the sauce over the warm chicken and serve at once.

Clarified Butter

To clarify butter melt unsalted butter completely over low heat. Remove and allow the milk solids to settle to the bottom. There will still be some white foam on top. Strain the butter through a sieve lined with two thicknesses of rinsed and squeezed cheesecloth into a bowl; the milky solids will be left behind the pan. Pour into a jar or crock and store, covered, in the refrigerator. Use as you would butter for recipes that require sautéing or light browning.

Clarified butter is similar to the *ghee* used in Middle Eastern cooking, but it is prepared in a shorter time. Ghee is made by allowing the melted butter to simmer for about an hour or until the milk solids turn brown. Because there is no moisture left in clarified butter or ghee, it can never go rancid, and thus is used for cooking in hot climates.

Hunan-Style Smoked Chicken

Nina Simonds instructed us in wok cooking and it was from her I learned that a wok has many uses beyond the traditional one. Here, it is used to smoke and cook a chicken. (Serves 6)

Ingredients

1   whole frying chicken, about 2½–3 pounds

Mixture 1

2   tablespoons rice wine
2   teaspoons salt
3   stalks scallions, smashed
2   slices ginger root, smashed

½   tablespoon whole Szechuan peppercorns (available in Chinese food store)

Mixture 2

4   tablespoons black tea leaves
2   tablespoons brown sugar

1   teaspoon anise seed
1   tablespoon sesame oil

Method

Rinse the chicken, drain thoroughly and remove any fat from the cavity. Rub the rice wine and salt of mixture 1 over the skin and inside the cavity of the chicken. Place the scallion stalks, ginger root, and the peppercorns inside the cavity and let the chicken marinate at least 4 hours, or overnight in the refrigerator. Place the chicken breast-side up in an ovenproof bowl or on a plate in a steamer and cover. Fill a wok with water reaching to the bottom layer of the steaming tray and heat until boiling. Place the covered steamer in the wok. Steam 30 minutes over high heat. Remove the chicken.

Cover the surface of a wok or a deep pot with a piece of heavy-duty aluminum foil. Cover the inside of the pot or wok lid with foil also. Place the ingredients of mixture 2, except sesame oil, on the bottom of the wok, then place a rack or two chopsticks, criss-crossed, over top, and the chicken breast-side up on the rack. (The chicken should be about 2 inches from the sugar-tea mixture.) Cover the wok securely and place over medium heat. After about 5 minutes, the tea mixture should begin to smoke. Smoke the chicken about 15 minutes, turning once. Turn off the heat and let the chicken sit covered for 10 more minutes. Remove the chicken and brush the skin with the sesame oil. Cut through the bones into bite-sized pieces, discarding the scallions, ginger root and peppercorns. Arrange the chicken pieces on a serving platter and serve.

Chinese-Style Stir-Fried Chicken

The more I learn of Chinese cooking, the more eager I am to "cook Chinese." Apart from the dishes that call for deep-fat frying, the Chinese method of quick cooking meats and vegetables is a nutritious one.

Traditional Chinese methods can be complex for a beginner and time-consuming for a busy cook, so here is my version for a quicker Chinese stir-fry. It can be used for chicken, veal, seafood, or fish.

Before you begin, be sure that you have the necessary ingredients as their taste is unique and crucial for success. Buy them in a Chinese or Oriental grocery store.

Essential
Medium soya sauce
Rice wine
Rice vinegar
Sesame oil

Optional
Hoisin sauce
Oyster sauce
Dried mushrooms

Pre-Preparation

Prepare the chicken mixture, the aromatic vegetables, vegetable mixture and sauce mixture ahead of time. Have hot rice ready. Cook the whole mixture just before you wish to serve it.

Ingredients

Chicken Mixture

2–3	chicken breasts, cubed	1	tablespoon sesame oil (if you like a lighter flavor use vegetable oil)
1	tablespoon rice wine		
1	egg white, slightly beaten		
1	tablespoon corn starch	½	teaspoon salt

Method

Cube the chicken, place the pieces in a bowl and add the rest of the ingredients. Stir, cover and refrigerate for at least 30 minutes. Heat 1 quart of water in a deep pan, add a drop or two of oil and bring to the boil. Place a colander in the sink. Just as the water simmers add the marinated chicken. Stir. When the chicken pieces turn white (2–3 minutes), pour them into the colander. The chicken can be refrigerated and kept for later.

Placing the chicken in boiling water is often omitted and instead, the marinated chicken is added to hot fat in the wok, and then removed before the final cooking process. I prefer the boiling-water method as, to my taste, the chicken tastes more tender.

Ingredients

Aromatic Vegetables

1	large clove garlic, peeled and chopped	2	thick slices ginger, peeled and chopped
		1	green onion, chopped

Method

Prepare, arrange on a plate and set aside.

Ingredients

Vegetable Mixture

4	stalks celery, chopped into uniform slices	1	zucchini, unpeeled, sliced thinly
5	small carrots, peeled and sliced thinly	4	water chestnuts, blanched with boiling water

Optional
6   dried Chinese mushrooms, soaked in boiling water, drained and sliced

Method

Prepare the vegetables and set aside together. These may be presteamed if you prefer less crunchy vegetables.

Ingredients

Sauce Mixture

2	tablespoons medium soya sauce	2	teaspoons cornstarch dissolved in 4 tablespoons boiling water (If using dried mushrooms or steaming vegetables use the liquid to dissolve cornstarch.)
1	tablespoon rice wine		
½	teaspoon sugar		
		1½	teaspoons sesame oil

Method

Combine all ingredients.

Ready to Serve? Begin.

Ingredients

3	tablespoons vegetable oil	½	teaspoon salt

Optional
1 teaspoon black bean, oyster or
   hoisin sauce

Method

Have everything ready. The table set, plates warming, rice cooked and hot, and all ingredients prepared and waiting.

Heat the wok until it is very hot and add the oil. Swirl over the entire wok. Toss in the *aromatic vegetables*, then the other *vegetables* and stir-fry actively for about 45 seconds so that they cook on all surfaces. Add the *chicken mixture*, season with salt, cover and cook for about 1½ minutes. Uncover, add the *sauce mixture* and continue to cook and stir about 1 minute more. Taste. Add more soya sauce if needed. If adding hoisin, oyster or black bean sauce, add now.

Note: To use this method for thinly sliced beef rather than chicken, omit the egg white in the marinade and the boiling water pre-cooking period. Stir-fry the beef in 3 tablespoons of oil and remove quickly just before ready to cook the whole dish. Add again after the vegetables are done as with the chicken.

Quick Chick

A quickly prepared chicken dish, geared to a small family but interesting enough for a guest or two. (Makes 2–3 servings)

Ingredients

3	chicken breast halves, boned and skinned, cut crosswise	1	tablespoon dry sherry
3	tablespoons oil	1	tablespoon rice vinegar or cider vinegar
1	onion, cut into 1-inch chunks	1	tablespoon soya sauce
1	green pepper, cut into 1-inch chunks *or*	¼	teaspoon hot pepper sauce
2	stalks celery, cut into 1-inch pieces	1	14-ounce (398 mL) can apricot halves *or* peach slices (unsweetened or light syrup)
½	teaspoon dry mustard	1	teaspoon cornstarch
½	teaspoon ground ginger	1	teaspoon water

Method

Sauté chicken in hot oil over medium heat until no longer pink. Add onion and green pepper (or celery) and sauté 3 minutes. Combine mustard, ginger, sherry, vinegar, soya sauce, hot pepper sauce and juice from apricots or peaches. Mix cornstarch and water. Stir into sauce and cook briefly until slightly thickened. Add apricots and heat through. Pour over chicken breasts and serve.

Quick Chicken Curry

A good curry is a meal in itself. The yogurt used in this one adds richness and a pleasant flavor. Serve with cooked rice and garnish with nuts, raisins and lemon slices. (Serves 4)

Ingredients

3	tablespoons light vegetable oil	½	teaspoon ginger
1	medium onion, finely chopped		Pinch of cumin
2	cloves garlic, minced	1	teaspoon salt
1	medium apple, peeled, cored and grated	3	tablespoons flour
½	cup finely chopped green pepper	1½	cups chicken broth
		2½	cups cooked chicken, chopped
2	teaspoons curry powder	1	cup plain yogurt

Garnish
Nuts, raisins, lemon slices

Method

Heat oil in skillet and sauté onion, garlic, apple and green pepper until well softened, then sprinkle with combined seasonings and flour, stirring to mix. Add broth and chicken and stir until thickened and heated through. Stir in yogurt just before serving.

Some spices, such as paprika, crushed red peppers, cayenne, and chili powder, occasionally lose their strength after a time. How can this be prevented?
For best results, spices should be kept in a cool, dry place and securely capped. Spices, such as those above, will deteriorate more quickly during the hottest times of the year. To protect them during those periods, keep them in the refrigerator. It is usually easy to tell when spices have begun to lose their flavor even without sniffing them, since they begin to darken in color. Ground spices generally lose their flavor more quickly than whole, but no spices will last forever.

Spanish Chicken

No one will say whether they prefer this typical Spanish soffritto served in pita bread, on brown rice or as the filling for a brioche (see page 81). It usually depends upon the time at your disposal for preparation and when you wish to serve it. It will take only ½ hour to prepare—but you must have some cooked chicken or turkey (leftover will do in a pinch) and the other ingredients in the house. For a quick supper try rice. For lunch use it to fill pita sandwiches. For guests, make the brioche. However you serve it, you need only add to it a light green salad—say, lettuce in summer, frozen green beans in winter. Poached pears, baked apples or crème caramel are light enough desserts to finish the meal well. (Serves 10)

Ingredients

3	chorizo or cotechino sausages, (about ¾ pound each) cooked and cut (if unavailable, use pepperoni)	1	cup canned tomatoes, drained and chopped
3	tablespoons olive oil	1	2½-pound cooked chicken, cubed
½	cup onions, finely chopped	½	teaspoon salt and pepper to taste
1	teaspoon garlic, finely chopped		
1	green or red pepper, sliced into ¾ inch pieces		

Method

Prepare the sausages by parboiling them in plenty of simmering water for 20 minutes. Cool and cut. In a large, heavy skillet, heat the oil. Add the onions, garlic and sliced pepper. Stir with a wooden spoon for 8 minutes or until the vegetables are soft. Mix in the sausage, then add the tomatoes, raise the heat and cook until most of the liquid has evaporated and the mixture is thick. Add the chicken. Taste and add salt and pepper only if necessary.

FISH

Fish Soufflé with Clamato Sauce

Maurice Pryor, instructor of chefs, prepares this light soufflé main dish as a simple but elegant example of low-cost cuisine. The clamato sauce is a pleasant accompaniment to any broiled or baked fish. (Serves 6)

Ingredients

1	pound halibut or sole fillets	4	egg yolks
¾	teaspoon salt	6	egg whites
¼	teaspoon freshly ground black pepper	1	good pinch tarragon
		1	teaspoon parsley
2	cups thick cream sauce (see below)		Juice of ½ small lemon
		1	cup clamato sauce (see p. 55)

Method

Purée the raw fish, salt and pepper in a food processor or put it through a meat grinder twice. Prepare cream sauce (below). Add tarragon, parsley and lemon juice to the sauce. Remove from heat and blend into slightly beaten egg yolks in a bowl. Stir in puréed fish. Beat egg whites stiff but not dry and fold ¼ of them into the fish mixture. Then fold in remaining whites gently to hold in the air. Spoon into buttered individual molds. Stand in a shallow sauce pan with 1 inch of water, on top of element and partially cover. Use a pot lid, slightly off centre, to accomplish this. Apply enough heat to just simmer the water. Do not boil. Turn out onto dishes and serve with clamato sauce.

Note: A few finely chopped raw shrimp added to the soufflé after cooking add a classic touch.

Ingredients

Cream Sauce

1½	tablespoons butter or blended butter	1½	tablespoons all-purpose flour
		1	cup milk

Method

Melt the butter in a saucepan, add the flour and stir over medium heat with a wire whisk until the flour is blended. Add the milk gradually, whisking vigorously and constantly until the milk is absorbed and the sauce is thick. Leave it over lowest heat for 15–20 minutes, whisking occasionally.

Ingredients

Clamato Sauce

10	ounces (290 mL) clamato juice	1	tablespoon flour
2	tablespoons butter		

Method

Boil clamato juice until volume is reduced by ⅕. Take 1 tablespoon of soft butter, add 1 tablespoon flour and blend together. Add butter and flour mixture to the clamato juice, a small amount at a time. Stir frequently. Bring to the boil and cook for 2 minutes. Add the balance of the butter. Season with salt and pepper. Keep warm until serving.

Italian Grilled Shrimp

If shrimp is reasonably priced in your neighborhood, buy it and prepare it *alla griglia* as the Italians do. The night before prepare the marinade and let it sit with the shrimp. For company serve with garlic spinach, risotto, and pears in port, or small chocolate mousse, for dessert. (Serves 4–6)

Ingredients

2½ pounds shrimp in the shell, cleaned and deveined

Marinade

1	cup olive oil	3	garlic cloves, minced
	Juice of 2 lemons	¼	cup parsley, chopped
	Drops of Tabasco to taste	1	teaspoon salt
1	tablespoon tomato paste		Freshly ground pepper
1½	tablespoons dried oregano		

Method

Wash and dry the shrimp. Allow to marinate at room temperature for at least 2 hours, or 8 hours in the refrigerator. Place in individual serving dishes if available, or an ovenproof dish to cook. Broil about 3 inches from the heat source for 3 minutes. Serve from the dish with the cooked juices.

Seafood Supper

Follow this recipe as it stands, or if you wish, alter it to suit yourself. You can present an original supper for friends even when the cupboard is almost empty.

If there is no chicken, use cornish hen. If neither is available, use canned clam juice as broth and omit the fowl. When fresh green peas are out of season, use frozen green peas, broccoli or beans. The only essentials are clams or mussels and an imagination. (Serves 4)

Ingredients

1	small boiling fowl or leftover poultry meat (2 cups) and the bones for broth	½	cup turnip, chopped
1	cup carrots, onion and other vegetables for broth	½	cup dry vermouth or dry sherry
8	cups water	½	cup peas, fresh or frozen
1¼	pounds fresh or canned clams or mussels	1	14-ounce can (398 mL) tomatoes
		½	cup parsley, chopped
		½	cup green onions, chopped

Method

Early in the day prepare a chicken broth using the fresh fowl, or the bones from a cooked fowl, the soup vegetables and water. Set aside. Remove the meat from the bones and cut into bite-size pieces. Place the broth in a large pot. Clean the clams or mussels very well. If using fresh mussels, scrub them with a brush until the water is clear with no sign of dirt or sand. Steam them for about 5 minutes over boiling water and remove. *Note:* Any mussels or clams that remain closed after steaming should be discarded.

Half an hour before serving bring the broth to the boil. Add the turnip and cook for 15 minutes. Add the balance of ingredients, including the chicken and seafood and continue cooking for a further 15 minutes. Pour into a pre-warmed tureen, or serve right from the pot.

Short Order Cooks

To a large can of hot clamato juice, add 2 14-ounce cans (398 mL each) canned clams, 2 cups leftover cooked poultry and other cooked, or frozen vegetables (e.g., potatoes, green beans, squash, cauliflower). Heat together, add sherry, garnish with minced green onions and parsley and serve.

Fish Casserole

This casserole is definitely company fare. The lobster adds a touch of luxury. (Serves 6)

Ingredients

1	pound frozen or fresh cod fillets	½	teaspoon salt
			Pinch of pepper
4–5	shallots or small green onions	2–3	tablespoons sherry
¾	cup milk	1	7-ounce (198 mL) can lobster
2	teaspoons lemon juice		Mushrooms, sliced and cooked
3	tablespoons butter		
2	tablespoons flour		Cheddar cheese, grated

Method

Poach cod fillets and chopped shallots in simmering milk in large pan for 10 minutes, or until flaky. Remove fish to oven casserole and sprinkle with lemon juice. Strain broth and reserve. Melt butter in a saucepan, sprinkle in flour, salt and pepper, and cook roux lightly for 3 minutes. Remove from heat, blend in reserved broth, gradually add sherry, lobster pieces and mushrooms. Spoon this mixture into oven casserole, mixing gently with the cod. Sprinkle with grated cheese. Casserole may be kept in refrigerator until required. Bake in 350°F oven, set inside a pan of water for 20–30 minutes.

What's the best way to freeze casseroles so they can be used quickly after work? Freeze them in the container in which they will be reheated. Line the casserole with heavy foil, fill it with the food and put it in the freezer. Remove the foil with the casserole after it has frozen, seal foil and return to the freezer.

Hot Salmon Sandwiches

Croque-Monsieur is a sandwich of cheese and ham that is very popular in Quebec. These sandwiches are variations using canned salmon. They are perfect for hungry teens or children at lunchtime. (Makes 6 sandwiches)

Ingredients

1	7¾-ounce can (220 g) salmon	12	slices bread, buttered
2	hard-cooked eggs, diced	3	eggs, slightly beaten
2	tablespoons celery, finely chopped	½	cup milk
2	green onions, chopped	¼	teaspoon salt
2	tablespoons cocktail sauce	1¼	cups potato chips, crushed
2	tablespoons mayonnaise		Butter, blended butter or margarine

Method

Drain salmon, reserving juices. Flake salmon and combine with the next 5 ingredients. Spread filling on 6 buttered slices of bread and top with the remaining slices. Combine eggs, reserved salmon juices, milk and salt. Dip sandwiches in liquid, then in crushed chips. Brown on both sides in a small amount of butter on a hot griddle. Serve immediately.

Yogurt and lemon juice replace mayonnaise and cocktail sauce for a reduced calorie (but not flavor) sandwich. (Makes 4 sandwiches)

Ingredients

1	7¾-ounce can (220 g) salmon		Salt and freshly ground black pepper
3	tablespoons yogurt		
2	tablespoons green onion, finely chopped	8	slices whole-wheat bread, buttered
1	tablespoon parsley, chopped	2	eggs, slightly beaten
1	teaspoon lemon juice		Butter, blended butter or margarine
½	teaspoon oregano		

Method

Drain salmon, reserving juices. Flake salmon and combine with next 6 ingredients. Blend thoroughly. Spread on 4 buttered slices of bread. Top with remaining slices. Combine reserved salmon juices and eggs, and dip sandwiches in egg mixture. Brown slowly on both sides in butter on a hot griddle. Serve immediately.

Supper-on-the-Run

This recipe takes virtually no time to prepare. If you have cooked rice in the refrigerator and a can opener in the drawer, you'll be barely in the door when supper will be ready. Cook plenty of extra rice; it's like reserve money in a savings account!

Ingredients

1	7¾-ounce (220 g) can salmon or tuna for every 2 servings	Soya sauce
	Cooked rice	Sesame seeds
	Frozen peas, beans, or other vegetable	Chopped green onion

Method

Set steamer rack in pan over 1 inch of water. Rinse tuna, if packed in oil. Place rice, tuna and vegetables in separate piles in steamer. Cover and steam until hot. Season with soya sauce. Serve on warm plates and sprinkle with sesame seeds and chopped green onion. If these aren't available, just look for something else—freeze-dried green onion, or chopped parsley. Relax and enjoy.

Broiled Salmon Muffins

Here is a fast and easy lunch or supper that's nutritious too. Just the thing for a busy day. (Makes 3 servings)

Ingredients

1	7¾-ounce (220 g) can salmon, drained	1	teaspoon lemon juice
			Freshly ground black pepper
½	cup creamed cottage cheese	3	English muffins, split in half (see p. 80)
1	small stalk celery, chopped		
1	tablespoon minced fresh parsley	½	cup shredded Swiss or Cheddar cheese
1	teaspoon Dijon mustard		

Method

Combine salmon, cottage cheese, celery, parsley, mustard, lemon juice and a few gratings of pepper; mix lightly. Toast muffin halves; divide mixture between halves. Top each with shredded cheese and broil briefly or microwave until cheese melts.

Note: If you are only cooking for one, prepare mixture and make only as many muffins as you can eat at one sitting. Refrigerate mixture and use the next day.

Salmon Cheese Bake

A nice lasagna using canned salmon, egg and cottage cheese. Nutritious and easy to prepare ahead of time for a late-night supper or buffet. (Serves 6)

Ingredients

1½	cups cooked rice	½	teaspoon salt
½	cup minced onion (1 medium-sized one)	½	teaspoon sugar
½	cup diced celery (1 stalk)	½	teaspoon oregano
1	clove garlic		Pinch of basil
2	tablespoons light vegetable oil	1	cup cottage cheese
1	7¾-ounce (220 g) can salmon	1	egg
1	19-ounce (540 mL) can tomatoes	2	tablespoons minced parsley
3	tablespoons tomato paste	4	ounces shredded Mozzarella cheese

Method

Cook rice according to package directions. In a large skillet, sauté onion, garlic and celery in oil until onion is tender. Flake salmon into skillet including juices and well-mashed bones. Add tomatoes, tomato paste and seasonings. Bring to a boil; reduce heat and simmer 5 minutes to blend flavors. In a medium-sized bowl combine cottage cheese, egg and parsley. In a 9-inch square baking dish layer half of the rice mixture, half of the salmon mixture, and then all of the cheese mixture. Then add remaining rice and top with salmon. Spread Mozzarella cheese over and bake at 375°F for 25–30 minutes or until bubbling around the edges. Serve immediately.

MEATLESS MAIN DISHES

Cottage Cheese

If you are ever in need of fresh cottage cheese or if you need a saltless, fatless cheese that is fresh and piquant, this recipe is simple and quick. Substitute lemon juice for the yogurt if none is available. Rennet is available in health food and drug stores. (Makes about 1 cup)

Ingredients

1	quart milk, skim is best but 2% will do	5	drops or ½ tablet rennet
2	tablespoons natural yogurt	1	tablespoon water
		½–1	teaspoon salt (optional)

Method

A container made of stainless steel, crockery or enamel is essential for setting cheese. I use a flat crockery bowl and place it in a frypan of water. You might use a double boiler. Slowly heat the milk and yogurt over simmering water until it registers body temperature. Remove from the hot water and add the rennet dissolved in the water—either drops or tablet. Cover and place in a warm spot for 12 hours, after which time a film of watery liquid should coat the surface of the congealed milk.

Line a colander with two layers of cheesecloth or a clean tea towel and pour the cheese into this. It should be resting over a bowl to allow the whey to drain through and be collected. Lift cloth from the colander after most of the whey has drained and tie ends to the tap so that the cheese can continue to drain over the sink. Other makeshifts can be arranged. (One of mine caused great hilarity when guests entered the bathroom where the cheese was draining!) When the whey has drained for several hours taste and add salt or fruits as desired.

Hint

Use the whey as liquid for soups or sauces. It's great for making bread, too. It contains minerals and vitamins.

Cheese Blintzes

(Serves 4, makes 12)

Ingredients

12   crêpes (see page 82)

Filling

1	pound creamed cottage cheese, or low-fat cottage cheese, drained		Cinnamon (optional)
		⅛	teaspoon salt
2	egg yolks	2	egg whites
2	teaspoons sugar	4	tablespoons clarified butter

Method

Prepare the crêpes (see p. 82) and set them aside while you make the filling. Freeze any you don't use.

Place the cottage cheese in a sieve set over a medium-sized bowl. With a rubber spatula press the cheese against the bottom and sides of the sieve, forcing it through. Scrape into bowl any cheese that is clinging to the outside of the sieve. Or place cheese in a food processor for a few seconds. Drop the egg yolks into the bowl of cheese, add the sugar and salt, and beat the mixture vigorously with a spoon until the ingredients are thoroughly combined. Taste the mixture; you may want to add more sugar if you prefer a sweeter filling. Some people like cinnamon, too.

Lay the crêpes out flat, browned sides up, on a long sheet of wax paper. With a small sharp knife, cut away the flap of each crêpe and trim off any scraggly edges. Divide the cheese filling among the crêpes, placing a mound just below the centre of each. With a fork, beat the egg whites until frothy. Lift the lower half of each crêpe over the filling so that its edge comes to the centre of the crêpe. Dip a pastry brush into the beaten egg whites and lightly coat the exposed sides and upper half of the crêpe. Then fold the sides in toward the centre and roll the crêpe forward, thus enclosing the filling securely and making a neat oblong package. Press your finger along the seam of each crêpe to seal it. Preheat the oven to 190°F. Line a jellyroll pan with a double thickness of paper towels to drain the blintzes and keep them warm once they have been fried, and place in the oven, together with the plates.

Pour 2 tablespoons of clarified butter into a 12-inch frying pan with a nonstick surface. Carefully place 6 of the blintzes, seams down, in the pan and fry them for about 3 minutes, or until their undersides are golden brown. Stand over them. They need attention as they are delicate. When the undersides are done, turn the blintzes with a wide metal spatula and fry the uncooked side. Transfer the blintzes to the paper-lined pan in the oven to keep warm. Fry the second batch of blintzes in the same fashion, transferring them to the jellyroll pan to drain the moment they are done. The blintzes will be at their best if they are served immediately on the warmed plates. They may remain in the oven for up to 10 minutes before serving. Serve with sour cream.

Broccoli, Pepper and Mozzarella Frittata

A frittata is the Italian cousin of our omelette. It is made by sliding the cooked, mixed egg towards the middle of the frypan with a spatula. As it moves, the uncooked egg runs to the pan's bottom where it gently cooks. A frittata is done when all the egg is barely set and golden. To serve, slide it onto a plate or, for dramatic effect, place the plate over the pan and turn the pan over. (Frittata is served at room temperature in Italy as part of the antipasta course.) (Serves 4)

Ingredients

- 1 cup broccoli flowerettes, rinsed and trimmed (save stalks for soup)
- 1 clove garlic, sliced
- 2 tablespoons butter or light vegetable oil
- 1 cup thinly sliced onion
- ½ cup julienne strips red pepper
- 6 large eggs
- ⅓ cup light cream or milk

- 1 teaspoon minced lemon rind
  Pinch oregano and dried rosemary
  Salt and freshly ground black pepper to taste
- 2 tablespoons butter or light vegetable oil
- ¼ pound Mozzarella cheese, diced

Method

Blanch broccoli for 3–4 minutes. Drain and refresh under cold water; pat dry. Sauté garlic in butter or oil in a skillet over moderately high heat for 3 minutes, remove with slotted spoon and discard garlic. Add the onion and red pepper and cook, covered, over moderately low heat, stirring occasionally, for 10 minutes or until onion is golden. Let cool. Beat eggs with cream or milk in a large bowl. Add the broccoli, onion mixture, lemon rind, herbs, salt and pepper, and mix well.

Heat a 7-inch omelette pan over moderate heat until hot, add 2 tablespoons butter or oil, and heat until hot. Add the egg mixture and cook for 5 minutes, or until the underside is golden. Scatter Mozzarella over the top and place the pan under a preheated broiler, about 4 inches from the element, for 1–2 minutes, or until the mixture is puffy and the cheese is browned slightly. Slide the frittata onto a heated serving dish and cut into wedges.

How do I use skim milk in place of whole milk in recipes?
For each cup of whole milk, use 1 cup of skim milk plus ½ tablespoon oil.

Le Fleutteur

A light luncheon or supper dish, this noodle casserole uses many egg yolks. It gives you the perfect excuse to make an angel cake or fruit meringue. Serve with a tossed salad of lettuce and green pepper slices. (Serves 4)

Ingredients

¼   pound thin noodles
1   bunch (4 cups) fresh spinach
½   pound Swiss cheese, grated
8   egg yolks, well beaten

1½   cups milk
½   teaspoon nutmeg
    Salt
    Freshly ground pepper

Tomato Sauce

1   onion, chopped
2   cloves garlic, minced
2   tablespoons olive oil
2   tablespoons flour
1   pound tomatoes, fresh, peeled, seeded and chopped (see p. 97)

1½   cups brown stock or a beef bouillon cube and boiling water
    Bouquet garni of thyme, bay leaf, celery and oregano
1   teaspoon sugar

Optional

¼   pound mushrooms, chopped
2   cloves garlic, minced
3   tablespoons tomato paste
    Parsley and basil, chopped

Method

Clean, steam, drain and chop the spinach. Cook noodles *al dente* for about 7 minutes. When cooked, mix together with the spinach, grated cheese, beaten egg yolks, milk, nutmeg, salt and pepper. Place in a buttered casserole or in individual casserole dishes. Bake for 35 minutes at 375°F in a pan of shallow water. Serve with Tomato Sauce.

Tomato Sauce

Sauté onion and garlic cloves in olive oil until golden. Add flour, blend and cook for about 2 minutes. Add tomatoes, brown stock, bouquet garni and sugar. Cook for at least ½ hour.

For an optional finish, sauté chopped mushrooms with garlic, combine with tomato paste, parsley and basil and add to the sauce.

Cheese-Stuffed Zucchini

Dieting is fashionable now. Magazines devote whole pages to recipes that encourage dieters to enjoy mealtime with this or that adaption of a standard dish. Serve this one with a clear soup for a starter, a light salad, melba toast with the entrée and fresh apple for dessert. (Serves 3–4)

Ingredients

8	zucchini, evenly sized		Small bunch chives, chopped
1	pound cottage cheese		Paprika
	Salt and freshly ground black pepper	1	orange (or 1 lemon)
8	ounces shrimp, peeled		Watercress

Method

Cook the zucchini lightly in a little boiling, salted water until tender, but still crisp, or, steam for 5 minutes. Cut the zucchini lengthwise and scoop out the insides. Be careful not to break the skins. Mash zucchini pulp with the cottage cheese and season well with salt and pepper. Fill the zucchini shells with the mixture, and put in a wide, shallow serving dish. Arrange the shrimp on top. Dust with paprika, scatter with chopped chives, and garnish with orange or lemon slices and fresh watercress. If necessary, these may be reheated in a 250°F oven for 15 minutes.

Eggplant Lasagna

This meatless version of the classic lasagna features a light tomato sauce with mushrooms and carrots, cottage cheese, and thin layers of steamed eggplant. It's redolent of Italian spices and reminiscent of rich, creamy lasagnas made with meat and béchamel sauces. Low, low calories in this dish! Serve with Country Kitchen Bread (p. 78), a vivid green salad and apple pie for dessert—perhaps plain, raw apples for dieters. (Serves 3–4)

Ingredients

1	small eggplant, peeled and sliced thinly	$\frac{1}{4}$	cup sliced, pitted black olives
1	tablespoon vegetable oil	$\frac{3}{4}$–1	teaspoon dried oregano
1	cup sliced mushrooms	1	cup 2% cottage cheese, drained
$\frac{1}{2}$	cup chopped carrots— 2 medium ones	4	ounces Mozzarella cheese, thinly sliced or coarsely grated
1	small onion, chopped		
1	cup canned tomatoes		
4	tablespoons tomato paste		

Method

Steam the eggplant slices for 5 minutes. Remove and spread over several thicknesses of paper towels to drain. Soften the mushrooms, carrots and onion in oil for about 15 minutes over low heat. Add the tomatoes, tomato paste and oregano, and simmer until the sauce is quite thick. This will take about 30 minutes. Add the sliced olives.

Lightly grease a casserole. There should be three layers of eggplant and four of sauce. Beginning with the sauce, spread over the bottom, arrange a layer of drained eggplant, then each of the two cheeses. Another layer of sauce, then the eggplant and cheeses. Finish layering with sauce. Bake at 375°F for 30 minutes. Let stand for 10 minutes before serving. Pass grated Parmesan cheese, if desired.

Lentil Casserole

Lentils contain more protein than any other vegetable and one 3½-ounce serving provides only 337 calories. For these reasons, as well as for their flavor, lentils should play a larger part in our diet. Serve with cooked brown rice and, if available, Fennel and Lemon salad (see p. 106). (Serves 4)

Ingredients

1¼	cups dried lentils	2	medium carrots, chopped
½	cup chopped onions	2	medium tomatoes, peeled and cut into quarters
½	cup chopped celery		
1	8-ounce (226 g) can tomato sauce	½	cup frozen peas
		2	tablespoons all-purpose flour
1	teaspoon dried oregano	½	cup cold water
4	cups water		Pinch of salt

Method

Rinse the lentils in a sieve, picking out any that look bad. Combine the lentils, onions, celery, tomato sauce and oregano with 4 cups of water in a heavy saucepan with a good lid. Bring to the boil, reduce the heat and simmer for ½ hour, checking and stirring occasionally.

Add the carrots, peas and tomatoes. Bring to the boil, then simmer covered for another 20 minutes. Taste and add salt, if necessary. Mix the flour and water together and add to the pot, stirring so that it is well mixed. Cook, stirring, until the sauce becomes slightly thickened. Taste again for seasoning.

Macaroni and Cheese

A traditional macaroni and cheese dish must have a light-textured pasta with a rich, thick cheese sauce adhering to every piece, topped with a crisp, cheesy crust. It has lost much character over the years, as cooks look for quick, inexpensive meals but should, in my opinion, be brought back to the place of honor it deserves. Macaroni and cheese—at least this macaroni and cheese—suffices as the main course in any entertainment. Serve it after a starter of Tomato Soup Portugaise (see p. 20) with a side vegetable salad. Lemon ice makes a perfect dessert. Follow with a tray of fruit, walnuts and coffee. (Serves 4)

Ingredients

½	pound (225 g) uncooked elbow macaroni		Salt and pepper to taste
2	tablespoons butter	4	drops Tabasco sauce
2	tablespoons flour	2	cups grated, sharp, old Cheddar cheese
2	cups hot milk or 1 cup milk plus 1 cup chicken stock	1	cup grated Parmesan cheese
		3	tablespoons dry sherry

Optional

Sautéed chopped onion
Dried mushrooms, washed, soaked, drained and chopped

Method

Cook the macaroni according to package directions, making sure that the texture is tender but not mushy. Drain and run under cold water so that the pieces will not stick together. Melt the butter, add flour and allow the flour to cook for a few minutes, mixing constantly. Add the milk, stirring rapidly with a whisk. Bring to the boil, stirring continually to allow sauce to thicken. Leave over very low heat for 20 minutes at a slight tilt—prop the pan with a pot lid so that one end lifts slightly—and collect the flour scum that forms. Throw this away. Taste, season with salt, pepper and Tabasco sauce and add optional ingredients. Now you are ready to layer the macaroni and cheese.

Choose a gratin dish that has a wide surface area, one that is broad and shallow rather than deep and narrow. The maximum surface should be exposed to the heat of the oven and the amount should fill the dish as close to the top as possible. Butter the dish and begin to heat the oven to 350°F. Combine cheddar and ½ cup Parmesan cheese. It is not necessary to complete the heating before putting the dish in the oven. Pour some sauce in to cover the bottom. Place in a layer of macaroni, then cheese. Pour more sauce over. Repeat this procedure twice more. Sprinkle

Parmesan cheese over top and bake for 35 minutes. About 10 minutes before the baking time is finished, pour sherry in and around the baked macaroni. Serve hot. This dish can be prepared ahead of time and baked when guests arrive.

Note 1: 4 ounces Parmesan cheese = 1 cup grated.
½ pound Parmesan cheese = 2 cups grated.

Note 2: Leftover egg yolks may be used to enrich the sauce. Whisk some sauce into yolks and beat lightly. Add this mixture to the sauce and whisk until smooth.

Buckwheat or Bulgur Casserole

Bulgur is wheat which has been parboiled, dried and cracked. Check the rice section of your supermarket or any health food or Middle Eastern specialty food store for supplies.

Buckwheat, kasha, or groats, are the fruits of the buckwheat plant. Look for coarse buckwheat when shopping. These grains can be used interchangeably. They are very nutritious, high in protein and B-vitamins and minerals. This recipe uses buckwheat groats, or bulgur. Serve it with Eggplant Lasagna (p. 66) or Sicilian Salad (p. 102). (Serves 6)

Ingredients

¾	cup celery, minced	¾	teaspoon lemon rind, grated
2½	tablespoons butter	⅛	teaspoon white pepper
1½	cups bulgur	¾	cup tomato juice
½	cup parsley, minced	2½	cups water
¾	tablespoon lemon juice	¼	cup walnuts, finely chopped
¾	teaspoon salt		

Method

In a large, heavy saucepan sauté the celery in 1 tablespoon butter for 5 minutes. Add the remaining butter and the bulgur and sauté the mixture for 3 minutes, or until each grain is coated with butter. Now, add the parsley, lemon juice, salt, lemon rind, pepper, tomato juice and water. Simmer the mixture, covered, over low heat for 30 minutes, or until the bulgur is tender but not mushy and the liquid absorbed. Stir occasionally with a fork to prevent sticking. Place the bulgur in a baking dish.

About 30 minutes before serving, heat the bulgur, covered, in a moderate 350°F oven for 20 minutes, stirring it frequently with a fork. Uncover the dish, sprinkle the top with walnuts, and bake for 10 minutes more.

Vegetable Casserole

I am often asked for lunch or light supper ideas—recipes that will be as delicious as quiche or casseroles but not as rich. This French gratin is a perfect answer, particularly in mid summer, when fresh greens overflow the market stalls. Begin the meal with fresh tomato vinaigrette, garnished with capers and red onion slices; finish with vanilla ice cream and fresh berries in brandy—a summer celebration. In winter, it is marvelous for a brunch party. (Makes 8 ample wedges)

Ingredients

14 ounces fresh spinach

5 ounces (1½ cups, loosely packed) fresh kale or Swiss chard, or 1-inch broccoli pieces

3 ounces (¾ cup, loosely packed) fresh sorrel leaves

5 green onions (1 cup, minced)

2 large zucchini (3 cups, sliced)

2 tablespoons fresh basil, chopped

1 clove garlic, minced

¼ cup fresh parsley, minced

Freshly grated nutmeg

Juice of ½ lemon

2 tablespoons olive or light vegetable oil

Salt and freshly ground black pepper

⅔ cup rice, uncooked

2 cups water

6 eggs

½ cup freshly grated Romano or Parmesan cheese

½ cup olive or other light vegetable oil

Method

Preheat oven to 350°F. Wash the spinach, kale and sorrel and chop. Steam the spinach and kale until just soft. Remove from the heat and strain well. Sauté the green onions and zucchini in oil (I like the flavor of olive oil here but you may use any light vegetable oil). In a large skillet add the basil, garlic, sorrel, parsley and nutmeg. Soften for 1 minute and then add the steamed spinach and kale. Taste, add lemon juice, taste again and season with salt and pepper. Remove from the heat. Meanwhile, cook the rice until soft. Mix well with the vegetables. Arrange this rice-vegetable crust in a deep gratin dish or 9-inch pie plate and bake for 20 minutes. The casserole may be refrigerated at this point and finished later on.

Beat the eggs, add the cheese. If casserole has been refrigerated, place it in a warm oven for several minutes. Remove from oven and pour oil over top, then pour in the egg-cheese mixture. Continue baking at 350°F until the eggs are set—about 30 minutes.

Hint

For a low-salt diet, substitute more lemon juice for salt.

Fettucine al Pesto

Pesto sauce has many variations but is always based on a combination of garlic, basil and pine nuts. This one comes from Genoa where the sauce is blended with a mortar and pestle. North Americans usually use a food processor. In this recipe the beans and potatoes are cooked with the pasta for a novel combination. (Serves 3 as a main dish or 4 as a starter)

Ingredients

Sauce

1   handful fresh basil leaves
1   handful pine nuts, lightly toasted in the oven
1   clove garlic
1   tablespoon Pecorino or Romano cheese, grated

1   tablespoon Parmesan cheese or 2 tablespoons if Pecorino is not available
    Salt
¾   cup olive oil, approximately

Noodles

2   quarts water
    Salt
2   medium potatoes, cut in halves
    Generous handful green beans, washed and topped

12   ounces fettucine noodles
    Parmesan cheese, grated, as a topping

Method

Sauce

Wash and dry the basil, add the pine nuts, the garlic, the cheeses and the salt. Blend them together adding the oil slowly. Just as you serve the pasta, add 1 tablespoon of its cooking water.

Noodles

Fill a stock pot with about 4 quarts of water, add salt. Put the beans and potatoes in boiling water and when they are almost cooked, add the pasta and cook *al dente*. Drain and place on a warm platter. Add the sauce, the tablespoon of cooking water and the Parmesan cheese.

Pizza Alla Neapolitana

Thanks to the food processor and heavy-duty kitchen mixer, bread baking has been simplified. That is not to say that homemade bread was ever difficult, but since several busy homemakers requested more information about using the new kitchen machines, this is a good example— simple and quick, low cost and delicious pizza. It will take 2½ hours to prepare with 2 of them spent away from the kitchen waiting for the dough to perform.

This recipe exactly duplicates the authentic pizza of southern Italy— crisp palatable dough with piquant, herb-spiced sauce. Serve piping hot or cold as an appetizer or main course. As a main course, serve a spinach salad with garlic vinaigrette, garnished if you like with sieved, hard-cooked egg. Follow this with poached apples or pears, almond cookies and coffee.

By the way, pizza in Italian means "tongs." So eat it with two fingers. It was never meant to be eaten with knife and fork. Freeze pizza unbaked. (Makes two 14-inch pizzas)

Ingredients

Dough

3⅓ cups or 1 pound (452 g) all-purpose flour

1 package (8 g) active dry yeast

1½ cups warm water, approximately

1¼ teaspoon salt

1 tablespoon olive oil

Olive oil for brushing on pan

Topping

2½ tablespoons olive oil

1⅓ cup puréed tomatoes

1 cup grated Mozzarella cheese

6 anchovy fillets (optional)

1 tablespoon capers

Sprinkle of salt

Pinch of freshly ground black pepper

1 tablespoon dried oregano

Method

Food Processor Method for Dough

Prepare the yeast as directed on the package omitting sugar. If using fresh yeast, dissolve it in ¼ cup lukewarm water (between 105–115°F). Measure 3 cups flour and salt and place in work bowl fitted with steel blade. Add oil to water-yeast mixture. Turn motor on and pour the warm yeast liquid in feed tube. Process for about 20 seconds. Add warm water in a drizzle very slowly while the processor is running. Add enough water to the bowl so that dough forms a ball that cleans the sides of the bowl; process so that the ball turns around bowl about 25 times. Let stand for

1–2 minutes. If this dough is sticky, add the remaining ⅓ cup flour, 1 tablespoon at a time. Process again for about 15 more turns around the bowl. It should now be ready. Turn it out onto a lightly floured wooden board and knead a few times. Form into a ball and place in a lightly floured bowl. Cover with a dry cotton tea towel and set aside for one hour in a warm, draft-free place.

Meanwhile, prepare sauce ingredients. Chop anchovies with the capers, grate the cheese and purée tomatoes.

The dough is ready when finger indentations remain and don't pop back. When the dough has doubled, punch it down to remove large bubbles, remove to a wooden board and divide into two. Preheat oven to 425°F. Lightly roll the dough, using a rolling pin or your hands, and smooth the dough to the shape of the pizza pan. I favor a round 14-inch pan of either terra cotta or aluminum. Brush the pans with olive oil. Place the dough on the pans, spread with ½ tomato purée, anchovies, capers, cheese and seasonings for each pizza. Place in the oven and bake for about 35 minutes. Cut into wedges and serve.

Traditional Method for Dough
Dissolve the yeast according to directions, omitting sugar. If using fresh yeast, dissolve in ½ cup warm water and let sit for 10 minutes. Place 1 cup flour in a large bowl and add dissolved yeast to the flour. It should be stirred well with a wooden spoon, then covered with a clean, dry tea towel and placed in a warm, draft-free place. It should stand until doubled. This takes about 1 hour.

Place the remaining 2⅓ cups flour in a large bowl and make a well in the centre. Add the yeast-flour mixture, the oil, salt and remaining 1 cup warm water. Using a wooden spoon, carefully begin to combine the ingredients, then use your hands to blend. Knead the dough first in the bowl and then on the board, until it is elastic—this will take about 10 minutes. Cover with a towel and let rest for another hour. Test for elasticity as described in food processor method. Proceed with the rolling and filling as above.

Lentil Ratatouille

When you need a vegetable dish that is colorful as well as different, try this. I like to have it around for those days when a simple, broiled fillet of sole or veal are on the menu. It can be served at room temperature in the summer as a barbecue accompaniment, but in winter, reheat it. Use any combination of vegetables that appeal to you and in any quantities as long as there are roughly 4 cups of chopped vegetables to go along with the lentils and potatoes. Chop the vegetables so that they are all about the same size. Dieters should omit the olive oil and soften the onion in chicken broth or tomato juice. (Serves 4)

Ingredients

1	cup potato, cooked and cubed	2	stalks celery, chopped
½	cup dry lentils	3	green onions, chopped
	Water	1	leek, chopped
1	tablespoon light vegetable oil	1	clove garlic, peeled and chopped
½	cup onion, chopped	1	tablespoon lemon juice
1–2	zucchini, sliced thinly		Pinch freshly ground black pepper
2	tomatoes, peeled, seeded and chopped (see p. 97)		

Method

Clean the lentils by rinsing them well in a colander. Place them in a saucepan and cover with water. Bring to the boil and simmer until done, about 15 minutes or less.

Combine lentils and potatoes in a bowl. Heat the oil and soften the chopped onions until golden yellow. Add the vegetables and cook until softened. This depends on personal preference. I like them to retain some crispness. Combine the vegetables with the lentil and potatoes. Toss with the lemon juice. Taste, add pepper and if really necessary, a bit of salt.

Spinach and Ricotta Quiche

Any favorite vegetable may be used in place of the spinach. In the watercress season, I serve this with the cress as a base—finely chopped and placed in the crust before the filling. Broccoli is another attractive and delicious alternative. I often serve this dish as a starter for a special dinner, followed by chicken or beef sauté and stewed tomatoes. One memorable dinner in Rome, we had the cress quiche, followed by chicken livers al porto, risotto with fennel, and fresh tomatoes as the vegetable. Magnificent! (Makes a 10-inch quiche—6 servings)

Ingredients

1	10-inch quiche pastry shell, baked (see p. 77)	1	can (384 mL) evaporated skim, partially skim or whole milk
1	bunch fresh spinach or 1 package frozen	4	eggs
1	cup Ricotta		Pinch nutmeg
1	cup grated Parmesan cheese		Dash Tabasco sauce
			Pinch salt to taste

Method

Preheat oven to 375°F. Prepare spinach as package directs or, if fresh, by removing stems and steaming. Drain well. Squeeze out all of the water. Place all of the ingredients except ½ cup grated Parmesan cheese in the work bowl of a food processor and with the steel blade process until light and smooth. Taste and adjust seasoning. Pour into prepared pastry shell and sprinkle with remaining Parmesan cheese. Bake for 30 minutes. It will puff and brown nicely. Remove to a rack and let rest for 10 minutes. Serve hot or cold.

To Prepare without a Food Processor

Prepare spinach and combine with cheeses, reserving ½ cup Parmesan cheese for top. Whip the eggs, add the milk and combine with spinach mixture. Season. Pour into prepared pan and bake as above.

BREADS AND BAKED SAVORIES

Rich Pastry using the Food Processor

There are many recipes for pastry using the food processor. This is my favorite. Similar to a pâté brisée, it has the perfect texture for a moist filling such as quiche. Buttery in taste yet light, it balances superbly with cheese fillings. Cut calories in the filling by using skim milk or evaporated skim milk, but leave the butter for those first succulent bites of crust. (Makes pastry for a 10-inch quiche or pie.)

Ingredients

1⅓   cups all-purpose flour (untreated flour works best)

7   tablespoons chilled sweet butter or blended butter, cut into 1 inch cubes (keep in freezer for some moments before preparing)

¼   teaspoon salt

up to 6 tablespoons ice cold water

Method

Fit the work bowl with the steel blade and process the flour and salt until blended. Add the butter and process ON/OFF several times until the mixture is the texture of coarse meal. With the machine running, dribble the water through the feed tube, running the machine only long enough to incorporate all of the liquid and butter-flour mixture together. *Note:* Since the weather and absorptive quality of the flour determine the amount of water required, add water carefully and watch texture. The mixture will not form a ball but will be moist throughout. This can occur between 4 and 6 tablespoons of water. Form into a ball, wrap in plastic wrap and refrigerate for 30 minutes. Dough may be kept for one week in refrigerator.

Preheat oven to 425°F. Roll the pastry until very thin, fold and place over the quiche or pie pan and press into it. Trim edges and refrigerate. Line the pan with parchment or waxed paper, fill with dry beans in order to retain the shape and bake for 15 minutes. Remove beans and paper and bake for another 5 minutes. Remove to a rack and cool. Fill with any desired filling and bake according to those instructions.

Country Kitchen Bread

Here is an old-fashioned, crusty white bread—just one loaf for beginners. If you're expert at bread making, simply double the recipe. Have your plant-spray bottle ready, filled with water, to spray the loaf as it bakes. This gives a crisp outer crust reminiscent of farmhouse bread. (Makes 1 large loaf)

Ingredients

$2\frac{1}{2}$ cups unbleached, hard wheat, all-purpose flour

$1\frac{1}{8}$ teaspoons salt

1 tablespoon lard, shortening or butter

$\frac{3}{4}$ cup lukewarm water

1 teaspoon sugar

$1\frac{1}{2}$ teaspoons active dry yeast

Method

Mix flour and salt in a large mixing bowl and finely rub in the lard or shortening with your fingers. Dissolve the sugar in the water. Test the temperature of the water with your fingers; it should be slightly warmer than body temperature. Sprinkle the yeast over the surface of the water and leave for 10–15 minutes until the yeast has dissolved. The little pellets will fall first to the bottom, then rise to the surface one by one and explode to create a "head" of puffy foam. Add the yeast liquid to the flour all at once and mix well. Work with your hands until all the dry particles are gathered in to form a rough, slightly sticky lump of dough. Turn it out onto a clean dry surface and knead thoroughly. If the dough is too tacky and difficult to handle, work in only enough extra flour to make it manageable, but remember that the dough becomes less sticky as the gluten develops. Knead for not less than 5 minutes, preferably, for 10 minutes. When the dough has had sufficient kneading, it will have changed from a sticky mass to a smooth dough that feels elastic, no longer sticks to the counter, and has many tiny air bubbles under the surface.

To knead, push the part of the dough farthest from you with the heel of the hand, then pull and fold the dough back into the centre with the fingers. Turn the piece of dough by one-quarter and continue pushing, pulling, folding and turning, so that the whole of the dough receives equal manipulation.

Leave the dough to rise. If you are uncertain about rising time, do this: find a straight-sided container, a bowl, casserole or measuring cup that holds 4 cups exactly. Spread with light vegetable oil. Place the dough inside, turning it over and around so that the entire surface is coated with oil. A smooth surface is essential for a uniform bread. Cover this with a plastic wrap and a clean tea towel and allow to rise in a warm place. If the kitchen is cold use an electric heating pad, lightly wrapped in a towel and set at low, to surround the bowl. The temperature for bread should be no higher than 70°F, otherwise it tastes yeasty. When the dough mounds up to the top it is ready. This will likely take 1½ hours. If the room temperature is cooler than 70°F it will take longer. (If doubling the recipe, a 6-cup container will do.)

The dough is ready when two fingers inserted to the knuckles leave a deep impression. Test at the side, rather than the centre of the dough. If it is ready, lightly punch the dough down in the centre to release the air bubbles. Flatten the dough, bring all sides to the centre and form into a ball. Turn over so that folded ends are on the bottom. Cover again and set aside to rise once more. It takes slightly less time than the first rise. Test again with the fingers for lightness and proceed to shape the loaf. *Note:* If you wish, this step may be omitted but the loaf will not be as well textured.

When the dough has doubled in volume, turn onto a work surface. Knead lightly just to work out the large air bubbles, then round up the dough into a neat ball, cover with its bowl, inverted, and leave for 10 minutes before shaping. Then, flatten out the piece of dough using both hands until an oval shape is achieved, 11 inches long. Now roll up the dough like a jellyroll, roll back and forth to make quite smooth, then transfer to a greased baking tray and neatly tuck the ends of the roll underneath. Slip the tray inside a plastic bag and leave to rise in a warm place for about 45 minutes, until the dough looks puffy and wobbles when the tray is shaken. Remove the plastic cover and then cut a slash the length of the loaf with a sharp knife.

Preheat the oven to 400°F. Place a pan of hot water on the bottom shelf of the oven and put the bread on the shelf above. Bake for about 35 minutes, spraying with water 3 times during baking time. If you prefer a less crisp crust, omit the pan of water and spraying. Brown on the outside, the loaf will make a hollow sound when tapped with your knuckles. This means it is done and ready to cool on a wire rack.

Method for a Kitchen Machine with Dough Hook Attachment
Prepare the dough using the same ingredients and following the kneading method that comes in the instruction manual for your machine.

Note: Never knead at a speed above 2 or 3 on your machine. Continue with the same rising and shaping method described for hand-kneaded bread.

Food Processor Method
Combine 2¼ cups flour, salt and lard, in work bowl fitted with the steel knife. Keep ¼ cup flour reserved for addition later, if it is needed. Dissolve yeast in ¼ cup warm water to which sugar has been added. Reserve ½ cup *cold* water. (The blades travel at such high speed, that it is

possible to raise the temperature some degrees more than is beneficial for the yeast.)

Process, using ON/OFF switch to combine flour, salt and fat. Add yeast solution. Process ON/OFF quickly. Add cold water through feed tube and process ON/OFF until dough forms a ball. If it is too sticky, i.e., it sticks to the fingers—add more flour until it forms a sticky but not glue-like ball of dough. This whole process will take under 60 seconds. Remove dough, knead for a minute by hand to smooth the dough and return to greased work bowl to rise. Follow the rising and shaping instructions for hand-kneaded dough.

Note: If you plan to double the recipe, remember to use the plastic dough blade. Manufacturers advise that you use this blade for any amount greater than 3½ cups flour.

English Muffins

A joy to make and a treat to eat. Serve with butter, jam or honey. (Makes about 20 muffins)

Ingredients

1	teaspoon sugar	2	tablespoons sugar
1	cup warm water	¼	cup shortening
1	package (8 g) active dry yeast	5½-6	cups all-purpose flour
1	cup scalded milk		Cornmeal
1	teaspoon salt		

Method

Dissolve 1 teaspoon sugar in warm water. Sprinkle with yeast and allow to stand 10 minutes.

Combine milk, salt, sugar and shortening in a large bowl. Stir to melt shortening. Cool to lukewarm. Add yeast mixture and beat in 3 cups flour. Gradually add another 2½ to 3 cups flour to make a stiff dough. Turn dough out onto lightly floured board and knead 8-10 minutes. Shape into a smooth ball and place in a greased bowl, rotating dough to grease surface. Cover and let rise until dough doubles (about 1 hour). Punch down and turn onto lightly floured board and roll to ½ inch thick. Cut with floured 3-4 inch round cookie cutter. Place on baking sheets sprinkled with cornmeal. Brush tops with water. Sprinkle with cornmeal. Cover and let rise until doubled (about 40 minutes). Fry over low heat, in lightly greased uncovered frying pan for 5-8 minutes on each side or bake in preheated 450°F oven 5-8 minutes on each side.

Brioche

Making a brioche is time consuming. If you plan to fill it with Spanish Chicken (see p. 52) for Sunday supper, prepare the brioche mixture on Saturday morning, let it rise twice and then refrigerate it with a weight on top so it won't rise too far, too fast. Then, 2 hours before serving on Sunday, bring it out, let it adjust for 1 hour to room temperature. Roll it, fit it, fill, cover, raise and bake it. That way, there is no last minute rush! This brioche makes a 12-inch pie—about the size of a medium pizza. (Serves 10)

Ingredients

1	package (8 g) active dry yeast		1	tablespoon olive oil
	Pinch sugar		1	egg, lightly beaten
½	cup lukewarm water			Olive oil
2½–3	cups all-purpose flour		1	egg yolk, for brushing on crust
1	teaspoon salt			
½	cup lukewarm milk			

Method

Mix the yeast, sugar and the warm water together. Place 2½ cups of the flour in a large mixing bowl. Add the salt and stir. When the yeast mixture starts to foam add it to the flour mixture. Add milk, oil and egg. Stir all the ingredients with a wooden spoon until the flour has absorbed all the liquid. Place the dough on a lightly floured surface. Knead the dough by pushing it forward and folding it in half on top of itself. Repeat the kneading for about 10 minutes or until the dough is smooth. Place the dough in a large bowl that has been spread with olive oil. Turn the dough in the bowl so it will be lightly coated with oil. Let the dough rise until double in bulk (about 1 hour). After the dough has risen, punch it down with your fist to its original size. Allow the dough to rise again.

Spread a large cookie sheet with melted butter. Roll half the dough on the sheet until it measures 12 inches in diameter. Spread the desired filling mixture over the dough to within 1½ inches of the edge. Avoid spilling any filling on outer edge, or it will be difficult to seal. Brush pastry rim with egg yolk. Roll the other half of the dough to 13 inches and place over the top, sealing edges with your fingers. Then seal using the tines of a fork. Glaze the top crust twice with egg yolk, both before and after rising. Cut a hole in the centre of the pie about ½ inch in diameter. Allow the pie to rise for 20 minutes. Bake at 350°F for 30 minutes, or until brown. When nicely browned, cool on a rack. Cut into wedges to serve.

Main Course Crêpes
(Makes 16–18 crêpes, 6 inches in diameter)

Ingredients

¾ cup milk	3 tablespoons light vegetable oil, such as safflower, sunflower or corn
¾ cup water	
3 eggs	
1½ cups all-purpose flour	2 tablespoons clarified butter, melted (see p. 46)
¼ teaspoon salt	

Method

Food Processor or Blender Method
Combine the milk, water, eggs, flour, salt and oil in the blender or food processor. Cover with plastic wrap and let the batter rest, unrefrigerated, for an hour. After this time it should have the consistency of heavy cream. If it is thicker, beat in a teaspoonful of water. If it is still too thick, you may add a second teaspoonful, but no more.

Traditional Method
In a mixing bowl, combine the ingredients in the same order as the machine method, and beat them vigorously with a whisk for about 2 minutes. The batter will be fairly smooth, but to make certain that no lumps remain, strain it through a fine-meshed sieve into another bowl, rubbing any tiny lumps through with the back of a spoon.

Place an 8-inch, nonstick-surface frying pan with a 6-inch bottom over moderate heat. When the pan has reached the proper temperature (hot enough to skitter a drop of water across the surface), butter the pan lightly with some of the melted clarified butter using a pastry brush. Quickly lift the pan from the heat and hold it close to the bowl of batter. With a 2-ounce ladle or a ¼ cup dry measuring cup, scoop up about 3 tablespoons of batter and pour it into the pan. Tilt the pan from side to side until the bottom is completely covered. Immediately tip the pan and pour the excess batter back into the bowl, leaving only a thin film of batter clinging to the bottom of the pan. Return the pan to the heat and cook the crêpes for about a minute, or until the top surface loses its gloss. With a small spatula, loosen the flap, then invert the pan over a clean tea towel. The crêpe will drop out with its cooked side up.

Brush the pan with some of the remaining melted clarified butter each time, and make the rest of the crêpes in exactly the same way, piling them on top of one another, always cooked side up, until all the batter has been used. Use the crêpes at once for blintzes (see p. 62) or other filled crêpes, store, or freeze them. To store in the refrigerator (24 hours) layer each with a piece of waxed paper. Wrap in plastic wrap. To freeze, layer each and wrap in heavy freezer paper to keep airtight. Freeze for up to 4 weeks.

Brie in Brioche

Prepare the brioche recipe for Coulibiac (see p. 86) for this novel luncheon or brunch. (Serves 4)

Ingredients

1	pound round of Brie or Camembert cheese, with rind	1	egg yolk
1	recipe brioche (see p. 86)		

Method

Prepare brioche and when it has risen once and been punched down, place it on a pastry or marble slab and cut in two, with one part slightly larger. Preheat the oven to 375°F. Roll the smaller piece until it is 1 inch larger in circumference than the cheese. Place the cheese on top and pull the rolled dough until it is halfway up the cheese. Press to secure. Remove to baking sheet. Roll the other piece until it will cover the cheese and the sides completely. Dip a pastry brush into the egg yolk and paint the surface completely. Lay the top, painted side down over the cheese. Trim the edges at the base of the cheese neatly, all around. Cut a small hole in the top and brush with egg yolk. Place the wrapped cheese in the oven and bake for 20 minutes. Remove to a platter and garnish lightly with parsley and crab apples. Serve hot. This can be made ahead of time and warmed up for serving. Place in a 350°F oven for about 10 minutes.

Coulibiac

Coulibiac is a Russian specialty. It is a fancy dish of cooked salmon fillets layered between seasoned and sauced crêpes and cooked rice, wrapped in a rich brioche, baked to a golden color and served hot with clarified butter, usually at brunch and always for guests.

North American chefs have developed and perfected the recipe so that it can be made with North American products to suit that continent's palates. John Clancy, one of the foremost teaching chefs, demonstrated coulibiac to me and his class in the kitchen of his home in New York city. We stood around his marble-topped counter as the coulibiac was lovingly prepared and displayed. This is a work of art and requires care and patience—serve it with a simple cucumber salad marinated in yogurt with dill, and a chilled, sparkling, or light white wine.

Pre-preparation Schedule

Step 1. Prepare crêpe batter and allow to sit in refrigerator for 2 hours. There is little flour in the mixture so that the crêpe will be light and velvety. The holding time lets the flour expand to thicken the crêpe. Cover and store as described on p. 82. These may be made days or weeks ahead.

Step 2. Prepare salmon mixture 2 days ahead.

Step 3. Sauce should be made *after* the salmon, in order to use the salmon stock.

Step 4. Brioche may be prepared 1 or 2 days in advance.

Step 5. Rice mixture can be made on same day as salmon or brioche.

Step 6. Assemble, bake and serve the coulibiac.

Step 1—Crêpe Batter (10 crêpes)

Ingredients

⅔	cup all-purpose flour	4	teaspoons salad oil
2	eggs	¼	teaspoon salt
½	cup milk	2	tablespoons parsley, chopped
⅔	cup water	2	tablespoons dill, chopped

Method

Place the flour and eggs in a small bowl and beat them together to form a paste. Gradually beat in the milk and water. Add the oil, salt, parsley, and dill. Chill for 2 hours before using. Fry. See p. 82 for instructions on frying crêpes.

Step 2—Salmon Mixture

Ingredients

1	tablespoon unsalted butter, softened	1/2	pound mushrooms, thinly sliced
4 1/2	teaspoons shallots, finely chopped	2	tablespoons fresh dill, chopped
1	teaspoon salt	1/2	cup dry white wine
1/2	teaspoon black pepper, freshly ground	3/4	cup Sauce Velouté (below)
1	pound salmon fillets cut into thin slices, *or* striped bass, skinned	3	egg yolks
		1	tablespoon lemon juice

Method

Preheat oven to 400°F. Coat the bottom and sides of a 7 inch × 12 inch baking dish with the softened butter. Sprinkle the shallots over the butter and season them with 1/4 teaspoon of the salt and just a little of the freshly ground pepper. Cover the entire bottom of the dish with the sliced salmon. Place the mushrooms over the salmon and scatter them with the dill, 1/4 teaspoon of the salt and a little more of the pepper. Pour the wine over the fish and cover with a buttered piece of wax paper. Bake in the middle of the oven for 18 minutes.

Remove the dish from the oven and pour off all the liquid into a medium-sized, heavy saucepan. Allow the salmon to set at an angle (so the liquid runs away) for about 10 minutes. Add whatever additional liquid accumulates into the saucepan. Place the saucepan over high heat and allow liquid to reduce to 3/4 cup. Prepare the sauce (below) and simmer for 5 minutes. Beat the egg yolks together and whisk them into the sauce. Remove from the heat and stir in the lemon juice, the remaining 1/2 teaspoon salt and the remaining pepper. Spread this sauce over the salmon. Cover and refrigerate until the mixture is firm.

Step 3—Sauce Velouté

Ingredients

3/4	cup fish stock, or chicken broth	2	tablespoons unsalted butter
		3	tablespoons flour

Method

Melt the butter in a small heavy saucepan. Stir in the flour and cook for a few minutes. With a whisk beat in the fish stock or chicken broth. Bring the sauce to a boil to thicken. Reduce the heat to low and simmer for 5 minutes. Cover with wax paper and set aside.

Step 4—Brioche

Ingredients

½	cup warm milk	1	teaspoon salt
1	package (8 g) active dry yeast	6	egg yolks
	Pinch sugar	¼	cup unsalted butter, softened
2	cups all-purpose flour		

Method

Mix the milk, yeast and sugar together. Place the flour into a medium-sized bowl. Add the salt, egg yolks and the softened butter. When the yeast mixture starts to foam add it to the flour mixture. Stir all the ingredients with a wooden spoon until the liquid is absorbed by the flour. Place the dough onto a lightly floured surface. Knead the dough by pushing it forward and folding it in half on top of itself. Repeat the kneading for about 10 minutes, or until the dough is smooth.

Place the dough in a clean bowl that has been lightly buttered. Turn the dough in the bowl so that it will be lightly coated with the butter. Let the dough rise until double in bulk (about 1 hour). After the dough has risen, punch it down with your fist to reduce it to its original size. Cover with plastic wrap and place in the refrigerator until the coulibiac is ready to be assembled. If making some days ahead of time, place a weight over it so that the yeast cannot expand.

Step 5—Rice Mixture

Ingredients

1½	teaspoons minute tapioca	¾	cup chicken stock
¼	cup cold water	1	hard-cooked egg, sieved
1½	teaspoons unsalted butter	½	teaspoon salt
½	teaspoon onions, finely chopped		Pinch freshly ground white pepper
¼	cup uncooked rice (converted)		

Method

Cook the tapioca and water in a small saucepan for 5 minutes, stirring constantly. In a small saucepan melt the butter over low heat, add the onions and cook them until they are translucent. Stir in the rice until it is completely coated with the butter. Stir in the chicken stock and bring to a boil. Reduce the heat to low, cover tightly, and simmer for 20 minutes. Remove from the heat and stir in all the remaining ingredients with a fork.

Step 6—Assembly

Ingredients

1	egg yolk, mixed with 1 teaspoon cream or milk	1–2	tablespoons clarified butter (see p. 46)
½	cup freshly made breadcrumbs		

Method

Roll the brioche to a size larger than the pan holding the fish and sauce, about 11 inches × 18 inches. Lay 4 crêpes over the top of the brioche and spread with ¼ of the rice mixture. Cut fish mixture in half, lengthwise, and invert one-half over the crêpes, in the middle. The fish will be on top. Over this spread ¼ more of the rice mixture. Over this place 3 crêpes. Then, layer with another ¼ of the rice mixture. Then, the other half of the fish mixture. Place the last ¼ of the rice mixture on top of the fish. Cover with 3 more crêpes (10 altogether).

Roll one side of the brioche over the top, brushing with egg-yolk wash on the edges. Bring over the other half and seal. Turn the ends under and lay on a pan, seam side down. Cut a vent through the crust and the top layer of crêpes. Decorate by scoring the top surface with the blunt side of a knife. Brush the entire surface with egg-yolk wash. Cut a piece of heavy aluminum foil long enough to be wrapped round the brioche as a collar. Fold in half, half again, smooth against the counter, butter with a brush and wrap. The collar should just fit the brioche so that it doesn't spread outwards, but rises upwards. Secure with paper clips. Sprinkle the whole surface with the ½ cup of breadcrumbs. Allow to rise for 20 minutes. Bake at 400°F for 30 minutes. Remove collar and replace in the oven for another 15 minutes.

Remove from the oven and pour 1 or 2 tablespoons clarified butter into the vent. Place the coulibiac onto a serving plate. Serve with clarified butter poured from a sauceboat. Garnish with lemon wedges cut on an angle (wrap in plastic wrap if placing on a silver tray). Let sit for 10–15 minutes before serving.

To serve any leftovers place on a cake rack, and put into a roasting pan over a little water. Cover with a tent of aluminum foil and heat for approximately 10 minutes in the oven at 350°F.

VEGETABLES

Steamed Vegetables

This is a habit worth cultivating! A steaming rack for under a dollar is one of the best kitchen investments I know. Even so, you can improvise by using a rack of any kind in a roasting pan. Lift it from the water by standing it on pyrex measuring cups. The Chinese steaming baskets arranged in layers allow you to steam more than one vegetable at a time. This saves energy and burner space. Some cooks always prepare more steamed vegetables than are needed for a meal. The leftovers are chilled and added to a salad for the next day. Vegetables are at their best when they are fresh, slightly trimmed and steamed.

Just a hint to new mothers: when you begin to prepare foods for your baby, remember that steaming saves nutrients and time—no messy pots to wash.

Steaming Times for Vegetables

Asparagus spears, 10 minutes over simmering water
Green beans, 5 minutes over simmering water
Lima beans, 15 minutes over simmering water
Broccoli, 10 minutes over simmering water
Brussels sprouts, 10 minutes over simmering water
Sliced carrots, 5 minutes over simmering water
Cauliflower, 10 minutes over simmering water
Peas, 5 minutes over simmering water
Zucchini, 10 minutes over simmering water
Winter squash (½ inch slices), 15 minutes over simmering water

Sweet and Sour Carrots

(Serves 4)

Ingredients

2	tablespoons sugar		1	tablespoon light vegetable oil
1	tablespoon cornstarch			
2	tablespoons rice wine vinegar		10-12	thin carrots, cut in rounds
	Salt to taste		1	cup water

Method

In a small bowl mix sugar, cornstarch, vinegar and salt. Heat wok, add oil. Add carrots and stir-fry 3 to 4 minutes. Add water, cover and simmer for 5 minutes, or until carrots are tender, but not soft. When you hear sizzling remove lid and test. A little liquid should remain in the wok when carrots are ready. Add cornstarch mixture. Have carrots pushed aside. When cornstarch thickens, stir-fry carrots until crisp but tender, and serve.

Carrots in Cream Sauce

Rich and creamy, these carrots need attention—you have to add the cream gently as they cook. Prepare them for very special guests who appreciate fine taste in foods. They are different and delicious. Good with roast lamb, veal and chicken. (Serves 4)

Ingredients

1	pound carrots		Freshly ground white pepper
	Coarse salt	½	cup heavy cream
2	tablespoons butter		

Method

Cut tips off carrots at both ends. Do not scrape or peel them. Place the carrots in a large bowl of cold water and let them soak for about 15 minutes. Heat a large quantity of water in a flameproof casserole; add coarse salt. When the water reaches the boiling point, put the whole carrots into the casserole and let them boil until cooked but still firm (about 15 minutes). Drain and place the carrots in a large bowl of water to cool. When cooled, peel the carrots by gently pushing off the outer skin. Cut the carrots into small slices, about ⅛ inch thick. Heat the butter in a saucepan. When the butter is warm, add the carrot pieces and sauté for about 5 minutes. Taste for salt and pepper. Start adding the first tablespoon of heavy cream and stir slowly until the cream is absorbed. Continue to stir slowly and add more cream, a tablespoon at a time, until it has all been absorbed. Serve the carrots immediately.

Carrot and Onion Purée

Best served with beef, lamb or pork, this simple vegetable complements a plain dinner with verve. Depending upon what vegetables and herbs are fresh in the market, you can dress this up with different flavors. Try using chopped dill or parsley as seasoning; chopped nuts, caraway or toasted sesame seeds as a garnish. (Serves 6)

Ingredients

1½	pounds carrots (18 carrots, approximately, 4 inches long), washed and sliced	¾	cup warmed light cream, or milk with 2 tablespoons milk powder added
3	medium onions, peeled and quartered	3	tablespoons butter
			Sugar, salt and pepper to taste

Seasoning

1   teaspoon, choice of parsley,
     chervil, mint, dill, lemon juice,
     or a combination of them

Method

Steam the vegetables following general rules for steaming. When soft,
put them through a food mill or food processor fitted with steel blade.
Add cream (or milk) and butter. Taste and season with sugar, salt and
pepper. Whisk until smooth and well combined, then transfer to a hot
serving dish. This may be prepared ahead, covered and reheated before
serving.

Celery in Tomato Sauce

Celery is eaten raw so often that we forget it is delicious served hot. This
version of braised celery is especially good with a simple dinner of
scrambled eggs or a cheese soufflé. Broiled fish complements the flavors
here and I've even served it after a hearty cream soup with fruit, cheese
and wine to follow. Use the stalks only and save the leaves for a fragrant
soup—simmer them with chicken broth or dissolve cubes and blend or
process. Dieters should omit the oil: soften the onion in a fat-free pan,
adding a small amount of chicken broth if necessary. Trim the ham carefully until there is no visible fat. (Serves 4)

Ingredients

1   medium-sized celery head—
     about 1 pound
3   tablespoons light vegetable oil
6   small or 3 large onions,
     chopped
2   slices cooked ham, sliced into
     thin strips

1   small can tomatoes
     Salt
     Sugar
     Freshly ground white pepper

Method

Wash the celery, removing any blemishes, and slice into 2-inch pieces. If
they are wide cut them in half. Soften the onions in the oil in a low sauté
pan that has a lid and keep them cooking on low heat until they turn a
light brown. Add the ham, lay the celery overtop and pour on the
tomatoes. Cover and simmer for about half an hour. Taste, add seasonings. If the celery is not soft, continue a bit longer. If there is too much
liquid left, drain liquid to another pan and boil the juices down over high
heat. Pour over vegetables and ham and serve.

Corn Pudding

This is a good, hearty dish to carry outside for summer eating with ham or pork, chicken, duck, game or sausages. (Serves 8)

Ingredients

4	cups corn, about 8 large ears		Salt and freshly ground black pepper
3	tablespoons butter		
2	tablespoons flour	4	eggs, separated
3	cups milk		

Method

Scrape corn from cobs. Prepare a cream sauce by combining the butter with the flour in a saucepan; stir in the milk. Stir until the mixture thickens slightly, then combine with the corn. Add salt and freshly ground pepper to taste, and remove from the heat. Add the lightly beaten egg yolks and blend with the corn mixture. Cool slightly. Whip the egg whites until stiff and fold the creamed corn into them. Pour into a well-buttered soufflé dish or baking dish, and bake inside a pan filled with hot water (bain marie) at 325°F until the custard is just set—about one hour is usually sufficient.

Short order cooks can substitute 2 packages of frozen, whole kernel corn for fresh corn.

Sour Cream Onion Tart

Rich and delicious, this tastes best with steaks or chops that are prepared on a barbecue. (Serves 6)

Ingredients

1½	cups biscuit dough		Oregano
2	cups sliced onions	3	eggs, slightly beaten
4	tablespoons butter	1½	cups sour cream
	Salt		Freshly ground black pepper

Method

Make biscuit dough with a mix or with your favorite recipe. Press it into a well-greased 10-inch pie pan and flute the edges. Cover with sliced onions that have been wilted in the butter and seasoned with salt and oregano. Combine eggs with sour cream, add salt and pepper to taste. Pour over the onions and bake at 400°F until the crust is done and the tart is nicely browned.

Sweet and Sour Onions

Onions come peeled and ready to cook in the markets of Europe—so this onion dish is simpler to prepare there than here. To peel onions easily, plunge them into a saucepan of boiling water and boil for 30–60 seconds; the papery skin will just slip off. Use onions of 1-inch diameter or smaller for this dish. Serve with a meat loaf or sliced beef or, for an all-vegetable dinner, serve with Tuscan beans and crisp green beans. In Italy, these onions are served at room temperature as part of the antipasto course. (Serves 6)

Ingredients

$1\frac{1}{2}$ pounds small onions
1 teaspoon salt
Pinch freshly ground black pepper
$\frac{1}{4}$ cup butter
3 tablespoons sugar

$\frac{1}{2}$ cup white wine vinegar
1 cup chicken or beef broth— canned, homemade, or made with a meat concentrate cube

Method

Remove the outer skins of the onions along with the roots, taking care not to remove the root base as this holds the onion together. Pierce onions with a fork to help them stay whole during the cooking. Put all ingredients *except* the broth into a large skillet, the larger the better. (A 12-inch, teflon-lined skillet is ideal). Cover and cook on low heat for 30 minutes.

Add $\frac{1}{4}$ cup of broth and cook for 15 minutes. Add $\frac{3}{4}$ cup of broth and cook an additional 15 minutes, shaking the pan occasionally. Uncover and cook for about 5 minutes to reduce and thicken sauce. Taste to be sure the onions are done. If the centre is still hard cook for another 15 minutes, covered, adding $\frac{1}{4}$ cup more broth, if necessary. When finished they should be brown and shiny and coated with the sauce.

Hint

They may be cooked early in the day, covered and reheated in the oven or top of a double boiler for serving.

My vegetables need something to perk them up. Any suggestions?
Instead of discarding lemon rind when you've finished squeezing the lemon, drop pieces of it into the cooking water for frozen peas, carrots, string beans, broccoli or cauliflower. That'll do it.

Pumpkin Succotash

Here is a harvest favorite. Use fresh pumpkin or substitute hubbard, acorn or pepper squash. The blend of colors and flavors goes well with roast pork, pork chops or ham. (Serves 6–8)

Ingredients

4 slices bacon, chopped	1 19-ounce can (540 mL) tomatoes
¼ cup oil	1 cup uncooked, sliced green beans
½ cup chopped onion	
1 clove garlic, finely chopped	1 10-ounce package (283 g) frozen whole kernel corn, thawed
1 green pepper, seeded and finely chopped	
3 cups peeled, seeded pumpkin, or hubbard, acorn or pepper squash cut into ¾-inch pieces	2 teaspoons salt
	Dash freshly ground black pepper

Method

Fry bacon until crisp and drain. Set aside. Add oil to pan with onion, garlic, green pepper and pumpkin, and cook for 5 minutes, stirring occasionally. Stir in tomatoes, beans, corn, salt and pepper. Cover and simmer until pumpkin is tender, about 25 minutes. Serve topped with bacon pieces.

Cheese Potatoes

Just the dish to serve with broiled fish, or with kidneys, lamb or liver. Good too with cold baked ham. (Serves 6–8)

Ingredients

2 pounds potatoes, peeled	3 eggs, well beaten
1 clove garlic	Fine breadcrumbs
3 tablespoons butter	½ pound Colby or Cheddar cheese, grated
Salt and freshly ground black pepper	Melted butter

Method

Boil the potatoes and garlic clove together. Mash, add butter, salt and pepper to taste, and 3 well-beaten eggs. Butter a baking dish well and sprinkle with breadcrumbs. Spread half of the potatoes on the bottom, sprinkle with cheese, and top with the remaining potatoes. Brush with melted butter, sprinkle with more crumbs and bake at 350°F for 1 hour, or until brown and crispy on top.

Garlic Spinach

When spinach is young and the leaves are small and tender, or when you need to quickly dress a package of frozen leaf spinach, add sautéed garlic. It does wonders! You might try it with broiled or baked fish and carrots. (Serves 2)

Ingredients

1	pound, or 1 package frozen, spinach	Butter
1–2	cloves garlic	Salt and pepper
		Lemon juice (optional)

Method

Wash the fresh spinach several times or until there is no longer any sand left in the rinse water and the leaves feel smooth. Remove the stems and coarse sections from the leaves. Shake off water and set aside. Soften 1, 2 or more teaspoons butter in a pan with a lid. Lightly sauté the chopped garlic. When just yellow add the washed spinach, cover and simmer for 5 minutes. Remove from the heat, mix the buttered garlic throughout, add salt, pepper and lemon juice and serve hot.

To prepare using frozen spinach follow the instructions on the package, then toss with hot garlic butter.

Squash Purée with Nuts

A friend of mine serves this at family dinners to accentuate a roast. It has a crisp, sweet top and can only be served for special occasions. Creamed onions are a perfect match. (Serves 6)

Ingredients

3	pounds butternut squash, peeled, seeded and cubed		Salt and pepper
3	eggs, lightly beaten	½	cup brown sugar, well packed
¼	teaspoon nutmeg	¾	cup pecans, coarsely chopped
		3	tablespoons butter

Method

Prepare the squash by steaming, boiling, using a pressure cooker, or a microwave oven. When soft, purée in a food mill or processor with the steel blade. Add the eggs and process again. Taste and add seasoning. Transfer to a lightly buttered casserole and sprinkle with sugar. Top with nuts and dot with the butter. Bake at 375°F for 30 minutes. The top should be bubbly.

Scalloped Sweet Potatoes and Apples

This is a favorite fall-vegetable combination to serve with pork, beef, or as a side dish for broiled back bacon. Add some crusty bread and fruit and cheese for dessert for a nourishing meal. (Serves 6)

Ingredients

6	medium sweet potatoes, washed	½	cup firmly packed brown sugar
1½	cups sliced apples	¼	cup butter
1	tablespoon lemon juice	½	cup apple juice

Method

Cook the sweet potatoes in boiling, lightly salted water to cover until almost tender; drain. Peel potatoes and cut into crosswise slices ¼ inch thick. Toss apples with lemon juice. Butter a 1½-quart baking dish. Arrange half of the sweet potatoes in the bottom and cover with half of the brown sugar. Dot with 2 tablespoons of the butter. Add half the apple slices. Repeat layering. Then pour apple juice over top. Bake at 350°F for about 45 minutes.

Short order cooks can substitute canned sweet potatoes for fresh potatoes. Cut into ¼-inch slices and proceed as above.

Ratatouille Niçoise

Yet another version of our favorite Mediterranean summer salad, this one from Tante Marie in San Francisco. it uses vegetables that are abundant in late summer and early fall, so make as much as you can for storing in the refrigerator or freezer. It is delicious hot in winter. Serve hot or cold with meats, on toast, or in pastry shells. (Serves 4)

Ingredients

1	large onion, diced into small pieces	6	medium tomatoes, peeled, seeded and chopped (see p. 97)
2	medium green peppers		Salt and freshly ground black pepper
¼	cup olive oil, plus 2 table-spoons		Mixed herbs, such as tarragon, thyme, marjoram or bay leaf
2-3	garlic cloves, minced		
3	medium zucchini, peeled and diced into small pieces		
1	medium eggplant, peeled and diced into small pieces		

Method

Place onion and green peppers into large sauté pan with ¼ cup olive oil and cook until softened. Add minced garlic. After 1 minute add 2 tablespoons olive oil and the zucchini. Add eggplant and cook until softened. Add tomatoes and season with salt, pepper and mixed herbs. Cook until the desired thick consistency is reached.

To Peel and Seed a Tomato

Bring a small pot of water to a boil; drop the tomato in for about 15 seconds. Remove with a slotted spoon and peel. With a small, sharp knife, cut out and discard the core. Cut the tomato in half parallel to the stem end (not through it) and gently squeeze the tomato over the sink so that the seeds will drop out. Tomato seeds tend to make a dish bitter, and they are best removed. Once this has been done, simply chop the flesh.

Turnip Purée

Some purées are made with a thickened sauce such as béchamel or with cooked, mashed potatoes. This recipe uses cooked rice and is topped with grated cheese for a final browning under the broiler. A lovely vegetable for a single diner—just divide the recipe by 6 and cook in the toaster oven along with a small meat patty or fish fillet. (Serves 6)

Ingredients

3	pounds turnips, peeled and chopped	1	teaspoon dried thyme or marjoram
1½	cups cooked rice		Salt and pepper to taste
¾	cup warmed cream, or milk with 2 tablespoons skim milk powder added	¾	cup Swiss cheese, grated
		3	tablespoons Romano cheese, grated
3	tablespoons butter (optional)		

Method

Prepare the turnips until tender by steaming, using a pressure cooker, or microwave oven. Purée the turnips with the rice in a food mill, or processor fitted with the steel blade. Combine the purée with the cream, or milk, and butter. Taste; add herbs and seasonings. Transfer to a lightly buttered casserole and sprinkle with the cheeses. Before serving, warm in the oven then broil until the cheese is browned.

SALADS AND DRESSINGS

Dressings for Plain Salads

Dressings for plain salads are made with oil, wine vinegar or lemon juice, salt and pepper. Here are some different ways to season a plain vinaigrette.

Anchovy
Take 2 anchovy fillets (wash the salt off by running them under tap) rub through a sieve, or crush in a mortar or wooden salad bowl. Put them in the salad dish and add oil, vinegar and pepper.

Cream
Mix 4 tablespoons of fresh cream, not too thick, with a teaspoon of wine vinegar or lemon juice. Add salt and pepper.

Marseillaise
Crush a clove of garlic in the salad bowl; add oil, vinegar, salt and pepper.

Mustard Cream
Mix 2 tablespoons of Dijon mustard with 4 tablespoons of fresh cream; add a few drops of lemon juice, salt and pepper.

Remoulade
Crush or rub through a sieve 3 hard-cooked egg yolks. Put in the salad bowl and blend with oil, vinegar, salt and pepper.

Garnishes for Plain Salads

For green salads the most usual garnishes are aromatic herbs, such as chervil, chives, tarragon and sometimes parsley. These herbs are coarsely chopped or the leaves are picked from the stems and used whole. The following are also used to garnish raw or cooked plain salads.

Beets—cooked, peeled, cut into rounds, diced or in julienne strips

Capers—whole or chopped

Crusts of bread—rubbed with garlic and seasoned with a vinaigrette

Flowers—nasturtiums or violets

Hard-cooked eggs—cut in halves or quarters and chopped

Peeled tomatoes—cut in thin slices or quarters

Mushrooms—cleaned and sliced thinly

Salads and Their Dressings

Salads are either your strongpoint or they are not. Having a list of suitable dressings might turn you overnight from bored to inspired. Here are some suggestions that can be varied according to your taste.

Raw Salads	Dressings
Chopped celery	Vinaigrette
Celery in sticks	Remoulade
Celeriac	Remoulade
Curly or other endive	Marseillaise, remoulade with bacon bits
Kohl-rabi, coarsely grated	Vinaigrette or mayonnaise
Red cabbage, cut in julienne strips	Remoulade or vinaigrette
Green cabbage (tender parts cut in julienne strips)	Mustard cream
Cucumber, cut in rounds and left to stand in salt	Vinaigrette or cream
Cress	Vinaigrette
Watercress	Vinaigrette
Chicory	Remoulade
Fennel	Anchovy
Lettuces of all kinds	Vinaigrette
Romaine lettuce	Cream, Marseillaise or vinaigrette
Dandelion greens	Marseillaise
Leeks (green parts)	Vinaigrette
Radish (tender leaves and radishes chopped)	Vinaigrette
Bean shoots	Mustard cream

Cooked Vegetable Salads and Dressings

Cooked Vegetables	Dressing
Artichokes (bottoms)	Vinaigrette
Eggplant (rounds blanched in salt water)	Mustard cream
Artichokes (white and green)	Vinaigrette, mayonnaise
Beetroot (in rounds)	Mustard cream
Celeriac (cut in julienne strips)	Vinaigrette, remoulade

Cooked Vegetables	Dressing
Broccoli	Vinaigrette, yogurt
Brussels sprouts	Vinaigrette, yogurt
Rutabaga	Mustard cream
Kohl-rabi	Vinaigrette
Red cabbage (cut in julienne strips)	Vinaigrette
Zucchini	Vinaigrette
Spinach leaves (very lightly blanched)	Vinaigrette
Broad beans	Vinaigrette
String beans	Vinaigrette, yogurt with chopped nuts
Kidney and other beans	Vinaigrette
Lentils	Vinaigrette
Sweet potatoes	Vinaigrette
Leeks (white parts cooked in water)	Mayonnaise
Potatoes (cooked in water, cut up when hot and soaked in white wine)	Vinaigrette, mayonnaise
Parsnips	Vinaigrette, mayonnaise

Lemon Sesame Dressing

A chameleon-like dressing. The flavors are light yet distinctive enough to heighten any salad combination where a touch of lemon is called for. Goes well with a crisp green salad, tuna, chicken or fruit salad. (Serves 6—makes about 1 cup)

Ingredients

⅔ cup light vegetable oil, such as safflower, sunflower or corn oil
Juice of one lemon
2 tablespoons vinegar
2 tablespoons toasted sesame seeds
1 tablespoon sugar
½ teaspoon onion salt
Salt, if needed

Method

In a jar with a lid, combine all ingredients and shake well. *Note:* Lemon at room temperature gives more juice when squeezed.

Sicilian Salad

Pungent and interesting, this summer salad goes well with a barbecue or picnic. If fresh basil is not available, oregano may be substituted. (Serves 6)

Ingredients

½	loaf Italian bread	20–30	basil leaves, fresh
1	fresh onion	2	teaspoons salt
1	celery heart	½	teaspoon black pepper, freshly ground
1	small cucumber		
4	large, or 6 medium tomatoes, ripe but not mushy	¾	cup olive oil, or more
		⅓	cup vinegar, or more

Method

Slice bread thickly and soak in cold water for 15 minutes. Slice onion very thinly and soak in cold water. Wash celery heart whole, then slice thinly into a serving bowl. Peel cucumber, quarter lengthwise, dice and add to bowl. Dip tomatoes in boiling water for one minute, peel, seed, dice and add to bowl. Add shredded basil leaves. Drain bread, squeezing each slice to eliminate all the water. Crumble and add to bowl. Just before serving, drain onion on paper towels and add. Season with salt and pepper, add oil, vinegar, and mix well.

Kidney Bean Salad

Keep this recipe handy for a last-minute salad idea when hot dogs and hamburgers sizzle away on the barbecue—good with grilled liver or lamb chops, too. (Serves 4)

Ingredients

1	14-ounce can (396 mL) kidney beans, drained	½	cup onion, diced
1	large cucumber, diced	½	cup green pepper, diced
3	large tomatoes, diced and drained		Mayonnaise
			Chili powder
½	cup celery, diced		Bacon, crisp and crumbled

Method

Combine the kidney beans with the cucumber, tomatoes, celery, onion and green pepper. Dress with mayonnaise flavored with chili powder and sprinkle with bacon. Serve on crisp romaine.

Rice and Beet Salad

A colorful salad, ideal for cold buffet! (Makes 6–8 servings)

Ingredients

3	tablespoons light vegetable oil	3	cups cooked long grain rice, chilled
1	tablespoon vinegar		
¼	teaspoon tarragon leaves	2	green onions, sliced
	Pinch dry mustard	1	apple
1	teaspoon minced fresh parsley	1	teaspoon lemon juice
1	19-ounce (540 mL) can whole beets, drained and diced	¼	cup mayonnaise
			Minced parsley for garnish

Method

Whisk together oil, vinegar, tarragon leaves, mustard and parsley. Add beets, rice and green onions, toss gently and refrigerate several hours or overnight.

Peel, core and dice apple. Sprinkle lemon juice over apple and combine with mayonnaise. Spoon mayonnaise-apple mixture into rice mixture, toss gently but thoroughly. Garnish with minced parsley and serve.

Facts About Rice

1 cup uncooked rice weighs ½ pound
1 cup uncooked white rice gives about 3 cups cooked
1 cup uncooked brown rice gives about 2½ cups cooked

- If your cover doesn't fit tightly enough, you can make a good seal by cutting a piece of waxed paper slightly larger than the pot. Then punch a very small hole in the centre and put the waxed paper over the pot. Set the lid on this when cooking.
- Instead of placing a pot of rice on top of the stove to cook, cover the rice and place it in a 350°F oven for about 25 minutes, or until the liquid has been absorbed.
- To get light, individual grains of rice, moisten raw rice in a little hot butter or oil and stir over the heat until the rice whitens. Add some well-seasoned liquid of any kind until it reaches twice the height of the rice. Cover tightly and bake in a 350°F oven for about 20 minutes or until the liquid has been absorbed.

Chinese Asparagus Salad

This Chinese version of asparagus salad is a perfect accent to a spring-time Chinese meal. Serve with stir-fried liver or chicken, sweet and sour carrots or broccoli and steamed rice. (Serves 4 as separate salad course or 8 as a side dish)

Ingredients

1	pound young, fresh asparagus, stalks no more than ½-inch diameter	4	teaspoons soya sauce
		2	teaspoons sesame seed oil
		1	teaspoon sugar
		2	tablespoons sesame seeds

Method

Bend each asparagus stalk back until the tough root end snaps away. Discard ends. Slice remaining stalks into 1½-inch lengths. There should be about 3 cups of asparagus pieces. Wash asparagus under cold running water and parboil the pieces by dropping them into 2 quarts rapidly boiling water for 1 minute. Drain at once, and run cold water over the asparagus to stop the cooking and set the color. Spread on double thickness of paper towels and pat completely dry. This can be done ahead of time.

In a small glass bowl, combine soya sauce, sugar and sesame seed oil and mix until sugar is completely dissolved. Add asparagus. With a large spoon, toss to coat each asparagus piece thoroughly with dressing. Chill slightly—no longer than 2 hours before serving. Toss sesame seeds over top.

Zucchini Salad with Fresh Dillweed

A delicious cooked salad. (Serves 4)

Ingredients

1	pound small zucchini		Pepper
2	shallots, finely chopped (use some chopped Spanish onion, if desired)		Paprika
			Sugar
4	tablespoons olive oil	1	teaspoon dill seeds or 1 table-spoon fresh dillweed
	Salt	2	tablespoons wine vinegar

Method

Wipe the zucchini with a damp towel and slice thinly. Heat the oil in a sauté pan; add the shallots and zucchini and stir until lightly cooked. Add the seasonings and mix. Add the vinegar and continue cooking for about 5 minutes. Taste and adjust the seasonings. Turn out into an attractive bowl and serve at room temperature.

Cold and Spicy Cucumber Salad

For a Chinese buffet you can prepare this salad with zucchini or celery instead of cucumber. Cut the celery lengthwise with a potato peeler—it makes long, thin curls. Try this dish as a relish for cold meats or a fish salad. (Serves 4)

Ingredients

1	medium cucumber	1	tablespoon oil
2	tablespoons vinegar		Sesame oil
2	tablespoons soya sauce		Sesame seeds
1	tablespoon sugar		

Method

With a potato peeler, slice unpeeled cucumber into thin diagonal rounds. Blend vinegar, soya sauce and sugar briefly. Heat wok, swirl oil, add cucumber and stir-fry 1 minute only. Remove to serving plate, add vinegar mixture. Chill, covered, for several hours. Sprinkle with sesame oil and seeds before serving.

Dandelion Salad

This recipe is suitable for any tough-leaved greens, such as escarole and curly endive or a mixture of these greens. (Serves 6-8)

Ingredients

1-1½	pounds dandelion greens	2	hard-cooked eggs, chopped
5-6	slices bacon, diced		Freshly ground black pepper
1	clove garlic, crushed		
3	tablespoons wine vinegar		

Method

Pull the dandelion heads apart, trim the stalks, wash them thoroughly and dry on paper towels. Put the greens in a salad bowl. Fry the diced bacon until lightly browned, add the garlic and cook until brown and crisp. Pour the hot bacon and fat over the salad greens and toss until they wilt slightly. (The French call it *fatiguer*, 'to tire'.) Add the vinegar to the pan, heat and stir to dissolve any pan juices and pour over the greens. Add the hard-cooked eggs, plenty of pepper and toss. Taste for seasoning—if the bacon is salty, more salt may not be necessary.

Green and White Bean Salad

This suggestion for a buffet salad is especially attractive on a table set for a barbecue. When field tomatoes are abundant and luscious, slice them onto a platter, top with a vinaigrette and slivers of green onion. Serve this salad beside them. (1 cup of mixed beans serves 1 person)

Ingredients

White beans, cooked or canned

Green beans, whole, blanched in boiling water for 1 minute, then chilled in cold water

Vinaigrette Dressing
2   parts olive oil
     to

1   part wine vinegar
     Salt and pepper

Garnish
Chopped chives, capers, shallots, parsley, hard-boiled eggs, green or black olives, dill pickles

Method

Pile white beans in the middle of a round dish and surround with whole green beans. Pour on vinaigrette dressing. Garnish with the chives, capers or others as they suit the main course; for example, use the dill pickles with spare ribs, parsley or shallots with chicken.

Fennel and Lemon Salad

When the menu is rich and full tasting and a light-flavored salad is called for, consider this one. Fennel comes on the markets in the fall. (Serves 4–6)

Ingredients

2   medium-sized heads of fennel
2   lemons plus 1 tablespoon lemon juice
3   tablespoons light vegetable oil

Sugar to taste
Salt
Freshly ground white pepper
1   tablespoon chopped parsley

Method

Using a lemon zester or potato peeler, remove the thin skin from the lemons. Avoid including any of the bitter white pulp under the skin. Slice into very thin, ribbon-like strips. Section the lemon into the salad bowl, squeeze the juice from the membranes into a smaller bowl for the dressing. Wash and slice the fennel into thin slices, beginning at the root end. Combine these slices with the lemon segments and strips of peel. Make the dressing of oil, lemon juice, sugar and salt and pepper to taste. Toss well. At serving time, combine with the chopped parsley.

Hint
I have often included other cooked vegetables in this salad—sliced potatoes, cut green beans or cooked broccoli flowers.

Cabbage and Fruit Salad
When the meal is a heavy one, choose this fruity, light salad. (Serves 2)

Ingredients

½	small white cabbage	1	tangerine or mandarin orange
	Olive oil or light vegetable oil (to moisten leaves)	2	tablespoons or more lemon juice
½	pound white and purple grapes		Chopped fresh parsley
1	firm apple		Chopped fresh mint, if available
1	sweet orange—seedless varieties are best		

Method

Trim the cabbage, wash and wipe well. Shred finely and toss with oil to moisten. Cover and chill in refrigerator.

Wash and prepare the fruit. Split the grapes and remove the seeds, slice and chop the apple into small cubes, peel and section the orange and tangerine. Add any juice that may be squeezed during the peeling. Combine the fruits and cabbage. Toss with lemon juice. Taste; it may need a little sugar. Serve in attractive bowls, topped with chopped parsley and mint.

Before peeling oranges or grapefruit for salads, heat them a few minutes in a hot oven. The white stringy inner fibers will come off easily when the heated skin is removed.

Yogurt and Cucumber Salad

This salad, popular in Mediterranean countries, is a refreshing companion to meat and rice dishes. It's good "hot weather food." (Serves 4)

Ingredients

3   cups thinly sliced cucumbers, peeled if desired

2   cups plain yogurt

2   garlic cloves, mashed

1   tablespoon mint or 1 teaspoon dried mint

½   teaspoon dillweed
Salt
Freshly ground black pepper
Lettuce leaves
Lemon wedges as garnish

Method

Put cucumber slices in a bowl. Mix yogurt with garlic, mint and dill and toss gently with cucumber. Season to taste with salt and pepper. Serve on lettuce leaves garnished with lemon wedges.

LOAVES, CAKES AND COOKIES

Jasmine Tea Bread

A different and delightful quick bread for afternoon tea. Your guests won't be able to guess the subtle flavor. (Makes 2 tea loaves)

Ingredients

¼	cup butter	1	teaspoon baking soda
1	cup sugar	½	teaspoon salt
1	egg		Pinch of cinnamon
1	tablespoon grated orange rind	½	cup orange juice
1	tablespoon grated lemon rind	¾	cup jasmine tea, prepared and cooled
1	tablespoon grated lime rind		
3	cups all-purpose flour	¾	cup chopped pecans
1	teaspoon baking powder		

Method

Preheat oven to 350°F. Cream butter and sugar together. Add egg and fruit rinds and beat well. Combine flour, baking powder, baking soda, salt and cinnamon. Add flour mixture to butter mixture alternately with combined orange juice and jasmine tea. Stir in pecans. Pour batter into 2 greased 9 × 5 inch loaf pans. Bake for 45 minutes.

Applesauce Honey Cake

This is a cake that will be cheered for its "real taste." It freezes well. Try serving it with a dab of softened vanilla ice cream. (Serves 8–10)

Ingredients

½	cup safflower, sunflower or corn oil	¼	teaspoon salt
⅓	cup honey	1	teaspoon cinnamon
⅓	cup dark brown sugar, packed	½	teaspoon nutmeg
1	cup applesauce	¼	teaspoon ground cloves
1½	cups whole-wheat flour	½	cup raisins (optional)
¼	cup wheat germ	½	cup chopped walnuts, almonds or pecans
1¼	teaspoons baking soda		

Method

Preheat oven to 350°F. Blend oil, honey, brown sugar and applesauce in a large bowl. Combine flour, wheat germ, soda, salt, cinnamon, nutmeg and cloves and add to applesauce mixture, blending thoroughly. Fold in raisins and walnuts. Pour into a greased 8- or 9-inch square baking pan. Bake for 35–40 minutes.

No Egg Carrot Cake

This is a moist spice cake. It keeps well, is an inexpensive finale to a meal and wonderful for those with allergies to eggs. (Serves 8–10)

Ingredients

1½ teaspoons baking soda	2 teaspoons cinnamon
¼ cup warm water	½ teaspoon nutmeg
1½ cups grated carrot (2 medium carrots)	½ teaspoon ground cloves
	½ teaspoon salt
½ cup plain yogurt	2 cups whole-wheat flour
1½ cups sugar	½ cup wheat germ
¾ cup safflower, corn or sun-flower oil	1 cup raisins

Method

Oil a 9 inch square baking pan and dust with flour. Preheat oven to 325°F. Mix baking soda with water and set aside. Mix carrots with yogurt in a large bowl. Stir in sugar, oil and spices. Add flour and wheat germ. Add baking-soda mixture and fold in raisins. Spread in prepared pan and bake for 1 hour, or until a cake tester comes out clean. Cool briefly, then turn out of pan and continue cooling on a rack.

Cinnamon Chocolate-Mousse Cake

This dessert tastes as good as it looks. Just the thing for a party buffet. (Makes 10–12 servings)

Ingredients

1½ 3-ounce (85 g) packages of ladyfingers	1 teaspoon cinnamon
	6 eggs, separated
1 12-ounce (340 g) package semi-sweet chocolate pieces	Pinch of salt
	½ cup sugar
½ cup water	1 cup whipping cream, whipped

Method

Line sides and bottom of an 8-inch springform pan with ladyfingers. Set aside. Place chocolate, water and cinnamon in top of double boiler, until chocolate is melted, stirring occasionally. Add egg yolks one at a time while double boiler is still over heat. Beat well after each addition. Remove from heat and set aside to cool to room temperature. Beat egg whites, salt and sugar until soft peaks form. Gradually fold chocolate mixture into egg whites. Fold in whipped cream. Pour into prepared pan. Cover and chill until firm, at least 4 hours or overnight. Remove sides of pan and decorate mousse with additional whipped cream if desired.

Honey Cake with Banana and Chocolate Chips

This is simply delicious. Make the four loaves and freeze any that aren't needed. To facilitate measuring the honey, oil the measuring cup first. (Makes four 7 inch × 3 inch loaves or two 9 inch × 5 inch loaves)

Ingredients

1¼	cups sugar	1	cup butter
2¾	cups cake and pastry flour	2	tablespoons diced candied orange and lemon peel
½	teaspoon cinnamon		
¼	cup butter	4	eggs
2½	cups chopped walnuts	½	cup milk
½	cup semi-sweet chocolate pieces	1	cup honey
		2	cups mashed bananas
2	teaspoons baking soda	1	teaspoon vanilla
1	teaspoon salt	½	cup ground walnuts

Method

Streusel Topping

Blend together ¼ cup sugar, ¼ cup flour, cinnamon, and butter until crumbly. Add ½ cup chopped walnuts and the chocolate pieces. Set aside.

Cake

Preheat oven to 350°F. Combine remaining sugar, flour, soda, salt and butter in a large bowl and blend until crumbly. Add remaining chopped walnuts and candied peel. Combine eggs, milk, honey, bananas and vanilla in another bowl and blend. Mix egg mixture gently into flour mixture until dry particles are moistened. Do not overmix.

Spoon batter into loaf pans that have been greased and dusted with ground walnuts. Sprinkle top of each loaf with streusel topping. Bake for 45 minutes or until toothpick comes out dry. Remove loaves from pans and set on wire rack to cool.

Change brick-hard brown sugar into syrup, instead of trying to soften it. In a double boiler moisten the sugar slightly with water and heat it until it dissolves. Add a few drops of both vanilla and maple flavorings—delicious!

Grease cake pans and casseroles the easy way by applying the cooking oil from a small bottle with a squeeze top. It's especially handy when only a small amount of oil is needed for frying.

Honey Sponge Cake

This light honey cake has a golden color and a fresh, nutty texture. I like it because it needs no icing, and for special occasions, a light dusting of sieved icing sugar makes it look festive. For a buffet, arrange overlapping slices on a platter. (Serves 10–12)

Ingredients

4	egg whites	2½	teaspoons baking powder
¼	teaspoon cream of tartar	1	teaspoon baking soda
¼	cup light vegetable oil	½	teaspoon salt
1	pound or 1½ cups honey	1	teaspoon cinnamon
1	cup sugar	½	teaspoon ground cloves
1	cup coffee, brewed and cooled	½	teaspoon ground ginger
4	egg yolks	¾	cup sliced almonds
3½	cups cake and pastry flour		

Method

Preheat oven to 350°F. Beat egg whites with cream of tartar until soft peaks form. Set aside. Blend oil, honey, sugar and coffee in a large bowl. Add egg yolks and blend thoroughly. Combine flour, baking powder, soda, salt, cinnamon, cloves and ginger. Mix into oil mixture, blending well. Fold beaten egg whites and sliced almonds into batter.

Pour into an ungreased 9- or 10-inch tube pan. Bake for 1 hour, or until toothpick comes out dry. Invert immediately until cool. Loosen sides of cake with sharp knife and remove to a platter.

If some egg yolk has dropped into egg whites, can anything be done to rescue them so that they can still be stiffly beaten?

If just a drop of the egg yolk has fallen into the egg whites and has not yet become mixed with them, it can easily be removed by simply dipping it out with the broken egg shell. But all is not lost even if the bit of yolk has blended with some of the whites. Use a small piece of soft white bread to move the part of the egg white containing the yolk over to the side of the bowl and up toward the edge. Hold it there, and pour the remaining clear egg white into another container.

Better than Mrs. Wilson's Oatmeal Cookies

"What's Cooking" couldn't be broadcast without our technical director, Hector Wilson. We often call upon him for comments on our recipe testing and this recipe passed as "better than his wife's . . ." but just. We hope we have her blessing for these cookies because they are wonderful—rich and crisp. (Makes 6 dozen cookies)

Ingredients

1	cup butter	1½	cups all-purpose flour
1½	cups brown sugar		Pinch of salt
1	egg, lightly beaten	1¼	cups oatmeal
½	teaspoon baking soda	1	cup desiccated coconut
1	tablespoon boiling water	½	cup nuts, chopped
1	teaspoon each vanilla and almond extracts		

Method

Preheat oven to 350°F. Cream butter and brown sugar until light and fluffy. Add egg and beat well. Dissolve baking soda in boiling water and add to the creamed mixture with vanilla and almond extracts. Combine flour and salt and stir into mixture until blended. Gradually stir in the oatmeal, then the coconut and nuts. Use a teaspoon to drop cookies about 2 inches apart onto a lightly greased cookie sheet. Bake 12–15 minutes.

Zucchini Oatmeal Cookies

If nutrition is your interest and cookies your downfall, try these cookies as the perfect solution. The whole grains are fibre packed, the vegetable and fruit are mineral rich, and best of all, they taste cake-like and delicious. (Makes 5 dozen cookies)

Ingredients

½	cup butter		Pinch of nutmeg
¾	cup honey		Pinch of ground cloves
1	egg		Pinch of salt
2	cups whole-wheat flour	1	cup rolled oats
1	teaspoon baking soda	1	cup raisins
½	teaspoon cinnamon	1	cup grated zucchini

Method

Cream butter and add honey. Add egg and beat well. Combine flour, soda, cinnamon, nutmeg, cloves, salt, rolled oats, and raisins in a separate bowl. Add flour mixture alternately with zucchini to egg mixture. Drop by teaspoon onto a lightly greased or fat-free treated cookie sheet. Bake at 375°F for 10–12 minutes.

Butterscotch Refrigerator Cookies

We like the nuttiness of these cookies—especially because there are no nuts in them. The bran cereal gives them crunch. I like to prepare them and keep them ready to bake in the refrigerator for those days when I need cookies but can't face the task of cleaning up. (Makes about 9 dozen 2-inch cookies)

Ingredients

1½	cups or ¾ pound butter or blended butter (see p. 2)	1	cup all-bran or grape-nuts cereal
2	cups brown sugar	3	cups all-purpose flour
2	eggs, lightly beaten	2	teaspoons baking powder

Method

Preheat oven to 375°F. Cream the butter and brown sugar until light. Beat in the eggs and stir in cereal. Combine flour and baking powder and add to batter. Shape into long rolls, wrap with waxed paper and chill. Slice and place 2 inches apart onto a greased cookie sheet. Bake for 10–12 minutes.

Whenever lightly beaten eggs are needed, shake them in a small shaker instead of beating them. It saves washing the egg beater.

Hamantaschen

You can make these filled cookies in any shape; the traditional one is triangular, however. They are made with joy in Jewish households in the spring, to celebrate the festival of Purim, when Queen Esther saved her uncle and the Jewish people from slaughter at the hands of Haman. Hence—Haman's hats or hamantaschen.

Poppy seeds are the traditional sweet for the filling, but often apricot or prune-jam filling is used instead. (Makes 3 dozen)

Ingredients

Filling

1	cup poppy seeds, if you can buy them ground, so much the better	2	squares unsweetened chocolate (optional)
⅓	cup milk	2	teaspoons lemon juice
⅓	cup sugar	2	teaspoons butter
¼	cup ground almonds	½	teaspoon vanilla extract
		2	tablespoons honey

Method

Combine poppy seeds and milk in a heavy saucepan; simmer and stir occasionally for 5 minutes. Add the remaining ingredients and simmer for a further 3 minutes. Cool and cover until ready to fill the cookies.

Ingredients

Cookie Dough

4	cups all-purpose flour	¼	cup ground almonds
4	teaspoons baking powder	½	cup vegetable oil
	Pinch of salt	1	cup sugar
	Zest of 1 lemon	4	eggs

Method

Combine flour, baking powder, salt, and lemon zest with the ground almonds and set aside. Blend the oil and sugar together, add the eggs one at a time and beat well. The mixture will be light and fluffy. Add the flour mixture.

Divide the dough into quarters, working with only ¼ at a time because the dough is very soft. Refrigerate the parts that are not being used. Roll the dough, adding more flour if necessary, until it is about ¼ inch thick. Cut dough with a round 3-inch cookie cutter. Place rounds 1 inch apart on a lightly buttered cookie sheet. Place one tablespoon of filling in the middle of each round and pinch the 3 corners together so that the cookie looks like a three-cornered hat. The filling will show in the middle. With your fingers roll each side of the triangle gently into the centre to contain the filling. Bake at 350°F for 15 minutes. Check often as they burn easily. They should be a light golden brown. Lift onto a cake rack to cool. Store in a covered tin.

Chocolate Mint Brownies

Mint brownies for a bazaar or sale—or just plain good eating at home. (Makes about 30 brownies)

Ingredients

3 (1 ounce each) (185 g) squares unsweetened chocolate
¾ cup butter
3 eggs
1½ cups sugar
1 teaspoon vanilla

½ teaspoon peppermint extract
¾ cup all-purpose flour
Pinch of salt
¾ cup chopped walnuts, filberts or pecans

Frosting

¼ cup butter
2 cups sifted icing sugar

2 tablespoons milk
1½ teaspoons peppermint extract

Garnish

⅓ cup semisweet chocolate pieces

2–3 tablespoons milk

Method

Preheat oven to 350°F. Melt chocolate and butter in top of a double boiler, or over low heat. Cool. Beat eggs, sugar and flavorings until light. Stir in flour, salt and nuts. Add to chocolate mixture, combining well. Pour into lightly greased 13 inch × 9 inch pan and bake for 25–30 minutes. Cool.

Frosting
Cream ¼ cup butter until light. Beat in icing sugar, milk and peppermint extract. Spread over cooled brownies and let stand until firm, about 1 hour.

Garnish
Melt chocolate pieces with the milk and drizzle over frosting. When set, cut into squares.

Filbert Meringue Bars

If someone you know is afflicted with a sweet tooth, these nut bar cookies will be ideal to serve with tea or a glass of milk. I use them as a treat for a drop-in buffet. (Makes about 30 bars)

Ingredients

½   cup butter
½   cup icing sugar, sifted
1   cup flour, sifted
½   cup currant or raspberry jelly, melted
2   egg whites

½   cup sugar
1   cup ground filberts—1 (85 g) package of whole filberts equals ¾ cup ground nuts
¼   teaspoon cinnamon

Method

Preheat oven to 350°F. Cream butter with icing sugar. Blend in flour. Press the mixture into a 13 inch × 9 inch cake pan and bake for 10 minutes. Let shortbread cool for 5 minutes then spread the top with melted currant or raspberry jelly.

In a bowl beat the egg whites with sugar until they are stiff but not dry. Fold in ground filberts and cinnamon. Spread the meringue over the jelly and bake at 350°F for 25 minutes. Let cool and cut into bars.

Date Balls

A quick cookie without turning on the oven! (Makes 18 balls)

Ingredients

2   cups bran flakes, wheat flakes or corn flakes
¾   cup pitted dates, chilled
¼   cup pecans
2   tablespoons honey

¼   teaspoon nutmeg
1   tablespoon butter
2   teaspoons lemon juice
Sifted or sieved icing sugar
18 pecan halves

Method

With food processor

Using the steel blade, process cereal, dates and pecans until an even consistency is reached. Turn into a bowl and combine with honey, nutmeg, butter and lemon juice. Knead by hand to blend. Shape dough into small balls and roll in icing sugar. Top with pecan halves.

With a meat grinder

Put the cereal, dates and pecans through a meat grinder. Follow instructions for processor for the balance of the method.

Torta Fregolotti

Torta Fregolotti means literally 'fragmented cake.' The word *fragola* is rooted in the Latin verb, *frangere*, which means 'to break,' hence the words fragment or fragile. Linguistics aside, this is a large crisp cookie. It breaks easily and Italians from the Frijole region eat the fragments with zabaglione or ice cream. Wonderful. (Serves 8)

Ingredients

1	cup plus 1 tablespoon butter at room temperature	2	tablespoons Aquavit, vodka or gin (in Italy, Grappa is used)
1	cup sugar	3	tablespoons lemon juice
2⅔	cups all-purpose white flour		Zest of 1 lemon, grated
1⅓	cups almonds, peeled and slightly toasted		

Method

Preheat oven to 350°F. Mix all ingredients together—it will not be smooth. Put into a buttered and floured 12-inch round pie tin with low sides. The mixture can be evened with a spatula. Place in the oven for one hour. Serve broken into pieces with ice cream or with whipped cream.

DESSERTS

Rhubarb Meringue Flan

Stratford, Ontario, can be proud of other accomplishments than its famous Festival. This flan, for example, was sent to me after I visited the restaurant on Albert Street called The Old Prune. It is a spring attraction that will be "held over" all year. (Serves 8–10)

Ingredients

1	2-pound (900 g) bag frozen rhubarb (fresh rhubarb in season is heavenly)		2	12-ounce (340 g) packages frozen raspberries

Pastry Base

⅓	cup butter		2	egg yolks
3	tablespoons shortening		2	tablespoons vanilla extract
3	tablespoons sugar			Water to form a smooth dough
1½	cups cake and pastry flour			
1	cup hazelnuts, coarsely chopped			

Topping

8	egg whites		1	cup sugar
1	teaspoon cream of tartar			

Method

Cook rhubarb just until soft, then add raspberries. Drain thoroughly, cool, and drain again. Preheat oven to 450°F. Combine, either by hand or with the dough hook of an electric mixer, butter, shortening, sugar and flour. Then add hazelnuts, egg yolks, vanilla and enough water to form a smooth dough. Press down dough into a greased and floured 9-inch springform pan. Bake in the oven for 20 minutes, until crisp, like short-bread. Cool.

To prepare the topping beat egg whites until they begin to stiffen, add cream of tartar and sugar and beat again to form stiff peaks. Spread the rhubarb and raspberry mixture over the pastry, about 1 inch thick. Then, layer meringue on top at least 2 inches high. Bake in a 400°F oven for 30 minutes until the meringue turns brown on top. We served it chilled, but it's also quite delightful eaten piping hot from the oven.

Rhubarb Apple Crumble

Apples and rhubarb have a great affinity. This is a family dish you'll love.
(Serves 4–6)

Ingredients

2	pounds rhubarb, washed, trimmed and cut into 1-inch pieces	1	teaspoon cinnamon
		½	cup rolled oats
4	medium apples, peeled, cored and thinly sliced	1	cup Graham cracker crumbs
		½	cup brown sugar
½	cup raisins		Pinch of ground nutmeg
¼	cup brown sugar	½	cup melted butter

Method

Place prepared rhubarb and apples in a well-buttered baking dish. Toss in raisins, the ¼ cup brown sugar and cinnamon. Combine oats, cracker crumbs, the ½ cup brown sugar, nutmeg and melted butter. Sprinkle over fruit. Bake at 350°F for 45 minutes. Serve warm.

Gin and Ginger Rhubarb Compote

Here's a rhubarb dessert with a difference. Try it and you'll be delighted.
(Serves 4–5)

Ingredients

1	cup sugar		Grated rind of 1 orange
½	cup water	½	cup orange juice
2	pounds rhubarb, washed, trimmed and cut into 1-inch pieces		Pinch of ground nutmeg
		½	teaspoon ground ginger
¼	cup gin	1	tablespoon finely chopped preserved ginger

Method

Dissolve sugar in water in medium-sized saucepan over low heat. Increase heat to high and bring syrup to a boil.

Add remaining ingredients, except preserved ginger. Reduce heat to low and simmer for about 10 minutes, until rhubarb is tender but not mushy. Using a slotted spoon, transfer rhubarb to serving dish and set aside. Increase heat and boil liquid 10 minutes. Pour this syrup over rhubarb and sprinkle with preserved ginger. Refrigerate until thoroughly chilled, about 2–3 hours before serving.

Apple Yogurt Dessert

One of the quickest desserts consists of a combination of condensed milk, lemon juice and a Graham cracker crust. This is a variation and improvement on the theme. The apples and the yogurt have a tart taste that is delicious. This recipe can easily be halved. (Serves 10–12)

Ingredients

¼	cup butter or blended butter (see p. 2)	1	cup yogurt
1½	cups Graham cracker crumbs	¼	cup lemon juice
		3–4	apples, peeled, cored and sliced into ¼-inch slices
2	tablespoons wheat germ	½	teaspoon cinnamon
1	can (397 g) sweetened condensed milk	¼	cup almonds, split and toasted

Method

Preheat oven to 350°F. Melt butter and blend with crumbs and wheat germ. Press into a 9 inch × 13 inch pan. Combine milk, yogurt, lemon juice. Set aside. Slice the apples and arrange them over the crust in an attractive manner. Pour the sauce over top and bake for 25 minutes. Remove to cool on a rack. Sprinkle with cinnamon and almonds. Chill in the refrigerator before serving.

Quick Apple Crisp

This is a short cut to a hearty apple crisp—granola makes a tasty topping. (Makes 2 servings)

Ingredients

4	tablespoons butter, divided in half	2	small apples
			Cinnamon and nutmeg
½	cup granola or glazed raisonola (p. 149)	2	tablespoons brown sugar (optional)

Method

Place a tablespoon butter in each of two 10-ounce custard cups. Melt in microwave or toaster oven. Meanwhile, pare and core apples, and cut into slices.

Place 2 tablespoons granola in each custard cup over butter. Arrange apple slices in each cup, sprinkle with cinnamon and nutmeg. Taste apple and granola—you may wish to add a tablespoon of brown sugar to each cup. Cut remaining 2 tablespoons butter into small pieces over apples. Top with remaining granola, bake 4–5 minutes in microwave or in a toaster oven at 350°F for 20 minutes until tender.

Baked Rice Pudding

A hearty rice pudding flavored with lemon rind, nutmeg and vanilla.
(Serves 6)

Ingredients

½	cup short-grain rice	1	teaspoon grated lemon rind
½	cup sugar		Pinch of ground nutmeg
4	cups milk	½	cup raisins
	Pinch of salt		
1	teaspoon vanilla	2	egg yolks (optional)

Method

Butter a 1½-quart casserole or baking dish. Combine rice, sugar, milk, salt, vanilla, lemon rind and nutmeg. Bake uncovered, at 300°F for 1 hour, stirring occasionally with a fork to prevent a skin forming. Add raisins and bake another 1½ hours, stirring occasionally.

For a richer pudding, beat 2 egg yolks lightly and add to the mixture before baking.

Variation

When the pudding is cooked, whisk 2 egg whites until stiff, add 1 tablespoon sugar, whisk again and pile this meringue mixture on top of the pudding. Place under a hot grill until the meringue is golden brown. Serve with cream and sprinkle with cinnamon.

Fruited Bread Pudding

This is a bread pudding for people who don't like them. The breadcrumbs gives a new texture and lightness to the dish. (Serves 6)

Ingredients

6	slices stale bread	¼	cup soft butter
¾	cup raisins, washed	½	teaspoon cinnamon
	Zest of one lemon or orange	¼	teaspoon salt
2	eggs	2	cups milk
⅓	cup sugar		

Method

Preheat oven to 350°F. Crumb the bread in a blender—or by hand, rubbing the stale bread between your fingers. Empty the crumbs into a greased 1½-quart casserole and add the raisins. Place the remaining ingredients into the blender jar and whirl for 20 seconds. Or, combine eggs, sugar and butter and beat until light. Add milk, salt and cinnamon. Pour into the casserole, stir to blend and place in a baking tray that contains some hot or boiling water. Bake for one hour.

Fresh Fruit Meringue

This is a perfect dessert to serve to calorie-conscious friends—a spectacular way to present a fruit compote. (Serves 6)

Ingredients

1 cup seedless grapes, sliced	Sugar
3 peaches, peeled, pitted and cut into large slices	2 teaspoons kirsch
	3 egg whites
2 pears, peeled, cored and diced	¼ cup sugar
2 oranges, peeled, sectioned and coarsely chopped	½ cup thinly sliced almonds

Method

Preheat oven to 425°F. In a bowl mix together grapes, peaches, pears and oranges. Sprinkle fruit with sugar to taste. Arrange the fruit in a decorative deep pie dish. Beat egg whites until they hold a shape. Gradually beat in the ¼ cup sugar and kirsch. Continue beating the meringue until it holds definite points. Place large spoonfuls of meringue over the fruit, or pipe on meringue peaks, each peak touching the next, until it makes a solid covering. Sprinkle with slivered nuts. Bake the dessert for 8-10 minutes, or until meringue is golden. Serve at room temperature.

To prevent fruit juice stains on hands, rub a little fresh lemon juice into skin immediately after the other fruit is handled.

Icy Yogurt Pops

Here are two ideas to please the young birthday party crowd. Yogurt pops are nutritious and flavorful. And faces on ice cream bring smiles to the faces of your little guests. (Makes 6 3-ounce cups)

Ingredients

1 cup plain yogurt
¾ cup frozen juice concentrate—lemon, limeade or grape

¾ cup milk

Method

Thaw the juice concentrate and combine with the yogurt and milk. Freeze in paper cups. When almost frozen, insert wooden sticks and allow to freeze until firm. When ready to serve, remove the paper cup by peeling.

Ice Cream Happy Faces

Super Mouse

Place scoops of ice cream on small plates. Press chocolate wafers into ice cream for ears. Make the face with assorted candies; e.g., gumdrops, licorice.

Circus Clowns

Place scoops of ice cream on small plates. Put a cone upside down on each scoop for the clown's hat. Make a happy face with assorted candies.

New York–Style Strawberry Ice

Ices, sorbets and frozen creams are the new desserts of the 1980s, but to prove there's little new under the sun, here is a description, printed in 1896 by Fannie Farmer, the dean of American cooking schools.

> Ices and other frozen desserts comprise the most popular desserts. Hygienically speaking, they cannot be recommended for the final course of a dinner, as cold mixtures reduce the temperature of the stomach, thus retarding digestion until the normal temperature is again reached. But how cooling, refreshing and nourishing, when properly taken, and of what inestimable value for the sick room!
> Frozen dishes include:
> *Water Ice*—fruit juice sweetened, diluted with water and frozen.

Sherbet—water ice to which is added a small quantity of dissolved gelatin or beaten whites of eggs.

Frappe—water ice frozen to the consistency of mush, in freezing equal parts of salt and ice being used to make it granular.

Punch—water ice to which is added spirit and spice.

Sorbet—strictly speaking, frozen punch—the name is often given to a water ice where several kinds of fruit are used.

Philadelphia Ice Cream—thin cream, sweetened, flavored and frozen.

Plain Ice Cream—custard foundation, thin cream and flavoring.

Mousse—heavy cream, beaten until stiff, sweetened, flavored, placed in a mold, packed in equal parts salt and ice, and allowed to stand three hours, or whip from thin cream may be used folded into mixture containing small quantity of gelatin.

By the above definition, this dessert is not, strictly speaking an ice. It has some heavy cream added to it. The orange juice brings out the flavor of the fruit in a remarkable way and gives the mixture an intensity of flavor not otherwise possible. The deep red color is the work of the frozen raspberries. According to Escoffier, a fruit juice ice with added whipped cream may still be called a sorbet or ice. Whatever its name, this type of ice is very light and delicious. (Makes 1–1½ quarts)

Ingredients

1 quart fresh strawberries, hulled	1 cup sugar
1 10-ounce package (283 g) frozen sweetened raspberries, defrosted and drained with juice reserved	¾ cup orange juice, approximately
	½ cup 35% whipping cream

Method

If you have a large food processor, prepare all of the ingredients at once. If you have a small one or a blender, process in 2 or 3 batches. Combine fruits, sugar and 1½ cups liquid. (Raspberry juice will comprise about ¾ cup and the balance will be orange juice). Purée until smooth and transfer to a large bowl. Beat the cream in a chilled bowl until soft peaks form, fold in the fruit mixture and pour into the cannister of an ice cream maker and continue according to manufacturer's directions.

Without an Ice Cream Maker

Refrigerate in a metal bowl for at least one hour. Then cover and freeze. Process when frozen and return to metal bowl. Cover and freeze. Repeat this twice. Remove from the freezer to refrigerator for one hour before serving. For a slightly less frosty mixture add more cream.

Lemon Ice

This type of ice is made in the Italian manner, in which a sugar syrup is boiled until thick and blended with a whipped egg white. It has a coarser, more full-bodied texture than a sorbet. In Italy, ices are served to clear the palate after a heavy meal; in France, they may do the same or are served as a starter course. However they are served, they are light and delicious and surprisingly simple to make. No special equipment is needed, although a food processor or blender makes the work easier. (Makes about 2 cups)

Ingredients

⅔ scant cup sugar
⅔ scant cup water
Zest of 3 lemons
1 cup lemon juice—approximately 4–6 lemons

1 egg white
¼ cup sugar
3 tablespoons water

Method

Prepare the sugar syrup by bringing the water and sugar to a boil just so that the sugar dissolves. Cool and refrigerate.

Remove the zest from the lemons using a vegetable peeler or special zester. Be careful to remove only the yellow skin. Allow it to soak for 1 hour or longer in the reserved sugar syrup. After an hour, remove the zest and combine the syrup with the lemon juice, mixing well. Pour the mixture into a 9-inch round or square cake tin, cover and freeze.

Meanwhile, whip the egg white until stiff. Dissolve the sugar in the water and boil for 7 minutes or until it begins to thicken. Candy thermometer temperature should read 225°F. Dribble the syrup over the whites, continuing to beat until the meringue is stiff and shiny. Refrigerate.

Process the lemon mixture for about 2 minutes in the food processor until the mixture is smooth and airy. Add the egg white meringue. Process ON/OFF 2–3 times.

Transfer the mixture to the pan again and freeze until partially set. Repeat this processing-freezing sequence twice. Then freeze. About ½ hour before serving, remove to the refrigerator. Spoon into chilled glasses. Garnish with frozen raspberries, strawberries or fresh, sliced kiwi fruit.

If you are using an ice-cream maker follow the method above, allowing the lemon juice–syrup mixture to freeze for a little under an hour. Turn machine off. Add the meringue to the almost frozen lemon mixture and continue to operate the machine until the ice is ready—probably another hour. Follow the machine instructions accordingly.

Crème Caramel

The French and Italian master chefs argue over the origin of crème caramel. My only complaint has been with its richness, but with this recipe I rest my case. It is not as rich as the traditional crème caramel, containing less cream and fewer egg yolks. (Serves 4)

Ingredients

½	cup sugar		Small sliver of lemon peel
2	tablespoons water	3	whole eggs
2½	cups milk	3	egg yolks
1	small vanilla bean	½	cup sugar

Method

Preheat oven to 350°F. Slowly, without stirring, melt the first amount of sugar with the water in a small saucepan. Then, turn up heat and continue cooking about 10 minutes until mixture is a dark caramel color. Watch carefully—it turns a straw color at about 150°F and darker at 180°F. Pour into a 1-quart heated, dry mold. Turn the dish around until the entire inside has been lined. Set aside. (Heating the mold is essential with glass or ceramic since the heat of the caramel might cause it to crack). Heat the milk with the vanilla bean and lemon peel to just below simmer and allow to steep. Meanwhile, beat the eggs and egg yolks in a bowl, then add the remaining sugar. Beat until light and foamy. Slowly pour in the hot milk, beating continually. Stir in 1 teaspoon vanilla extract here if vanilla bean is unavailable. Strain the mixture through a sieve into caramel-lined mold. Turn oven temperature down to 325°F and place the crème caramel in a bain marie and bake for about 60 minutes. Chill thoroughly—overnight is best. Unmold just before serving.

Is there any way of preventing the formation of a crust on cooked cream puddings? Try placing wax paper or foil directly over the surface of the partially cooled pudding. The covering should, of course, be removed before serving time. Crust formation can also be reduced by sprinkling sugar over the partially cooled pudding before chilling it.

Strawberry Soufflé

The flavor of this soufflé depends enormously on the quality of the strawberries, which should be highly perfumed. If they are not, add a little kirsch or lemon juice to the purée. (Serves 4)

Ingredients

1	quart fresh strawberries, hulled, *or*	½–¾	cup sugar
1	20-ounce (567 g) package frozen strawberries, defrosted, no sugar added	5	egg whites
			Icing sugar for sprinkling

Method

Purée the strawberries in a blender or work them through a sieve. You should have about 1½ cups purée. Add ¼–⅓ cup sugar, depending on desired sweetness. Butter the inside of a 1½-quart soufflé dish and sprinkle with granulated sugar, discarding the excess.

An hour before serving preheat oven to 350°F. Stiffly whip the egg whites. Add the remaining sugar and continue beating until the meringue is glossy and holds a tall peak. Stir a little meringue into the strawberry purée mixing it well, then add the purée to the remaining meringue. Fold them together as lightly as possible. Spoon the soufflé mixture into the prepared mold—it should reach the top of the mold— and bake for 25–30 minutes or until puffed and brown. The centre should still be slightly concave. Sprinkle the top with the icing sugar and serve at once.

Raspberry Soufflé

Substitute 1 quart fresh raspberries, or defrosted frozen raspberries, for the strawberries. Strain the raspberry purée to remove the seeds.

When a recipe calls for egg whites only, what are your suggestions for using the egg yolks?

Add them to scrambled eggs or poach them and use them in sandwich fillings. Use in meat loaf or instead of one whole egg in pancakes and French toast. Use 2 yolks plus 1 teaspoon of water to replace one whole egg in cookies or yeast doughs.

Freeze them by mixing them gently and adding one teaspoon of salt or sugar (depending upon how you plan to use them) for each one cup of yolks. Pour into ice cube trays. Freeze. Store in freezer bags. Thaw at room temperature and keep covered. One tablespoon yolks is equivalent to one yolk. Use them up in Le Fletteur (p. 65), Chicken Breasts

Florentine (p. 44), Crème Caramel (p. 129), Pear Tart (p. 134), Zabaglione Mousse (p. 136), Chocolate Pots of Cream (p. 140), Macaroni and Cheese (p. 68), Remoulade Salad Dressing (p. 99).

Grand Marnier Soufflé

Ignore anything I may have said before and consider this my favorite dessert. Luscious and moist yet light, the delicate flavor of this dish makes you feel downright sinful! Yet it contains only 122 calories for each serving (using 2% milk and 1 tablespoon liqueur) which is about the same as a cup of melon balls, a banana or a large apple. Be careful—if you're addicted as I am, one serving may not be enough! (Serves 6)

Ingredients

2	tablespoons flour or corn-starch	4	egg yolks
1	cup milk	1½	tablespoons butter
4	heaping tablespoons sugar		Grand Marnier to your taste
1	vanilla bean	5	egg whites
			Icing sugar for glaze

6 egg yolks – Beat in sugar
6 " whites 1 T. cream tarter
4 T Grand Marnier

Method

Moisten the flour first with a little cold milk. Boil the milk with the sugar and the vanilla bean; steep the bean for 5 minutes, remove, and mix the still-warm milk with the flour. Heat gently, stirring, just to the boiling point. Remove from the heat; the mixture should be very smooth. Off the heat add the egg yolks, the butter and the Grand Marnier. Up to this point the mixture can be prepared ahead, covered and kept until serving time—all day, if desired.

Add 1 tablespoon of the stiffly beaten egg whites to the mixture and blend well. Then fold in the remaining egg whites very gently so that they do not fall. Preheat oven to 325°F. Butter a 6-cup soufflé mold and sprinkle the inside with sugar. Fill the mold to three-quarters its capacity, smoothing the surface of the batter with a knife. Place the mold for 1 minute on the floor of the oven to heat the bottom; then place the mold in the centre of the oven. After 18 or 20 minutes, the soufflé should have risen 3–4 inches above the edge of the mold and started to take on a dark golden color. It should also begin to glaze. Quickly sprinkle the surface of the soufflé with icing sugar and replace the mold in the centre of the oven. In 2 seconds the sugar will melt; sprinkle again with sugar. Do this at least 6 times. You will get a beautifully colored, transparent, glazed coating. Place the mold on a platter and serve as quickly as possible. The guests should await the soufflé, never the reverse!

Reheat 1 hr Regrain oven at dessert time

Pears Cooked in Wine

This dessert is wonderful to have in your repertoire. If you are a single diner, eager for a delicious treat but too tired to begin lavish cooking after work, these pears can be made on the weekend and refrigerated. Remove them in the morning and leave them covered on the kitchen counter while you're at work. They will gather their full flavor by dinner time. If they are cooked just until soft, they will be infused with the most delicious pear flavor. They are best served at room temperature. For a special dinner party, prepare them ahead along with an almond or pistachio custard sauce. Make sure you provide guests with a spoon and fork for easy eating. To serve 1 or 2, simply divide the recipe by half. There will be an extra pear—save it as a bonus for a dull day. (Serves 6)

Ingredients

6	large, firm pears, preferably brown ones	1	slice lemon rind
4	cups dry red wine	5	tablespoons sugar
1	scant cup tawny port wine	1	cinnamon stick
1	cup water		Pistachio or Almond Custard Sauce (optional, see p. 133)
	Juice of half lemon		

Method

Peel the pears, leaving the stems on. Cut off a slice at the bottom of each so they will stand up when placed in a saucepan just large enough to hold them and not tip over. Stand them in the container, add the red wine, port, water, lemon juice, lemon rind, cinnamon stick and 4 tablespoons of the sugar. Cover the saucepan tightly, bring to a boil, lower the heat, and simmer for about 25 minutes, just long enough to cook the pears. Then leave them in the saucepan 10–15 minutes to cool, remove them, and stand them up on a serving dish. Remove the lemon rind and cinnamon stick from the pan, add the additional tablespoon of sugar, and cook again, reducing the liquid until it reaches the consistency of syrup. Watch the syrup closely as it condenses. It can burn rather quickly, so don't leave the pan unattended. Stir with a wooden spoon. The syrup will thicken enough to leave a space on the spoon when you run your finger through it. At this point, it is beginning to turn to sauce. Pour the sauce (it looks like dark red, liquid honey) into a cup. Cool a bit and taste. If it needs sweetening, add a drop or two more sugar. Pour over pears. Serve at room temperature.

Pistachio or Almond Custard Sauce

Ingredients

1¼	cups milk	2	egg yolks
1	small vanilla bean	¼	cup sugar
1	egg	¼	cup pistachios or almonds, lightly toasted

Method

Follow the method for Crème Caramel (p. 129) until the milk and egg mixture begins to thicken. Allow to cool uncovered. Leave at room temperature. Pour sauce over pears and scatter almonds or pistachios over top.

Fluffy Pumpkin Cheesecake

Crispin's restaurant in Toronto is justly famous for this super-rich cheesecake. (Serves 6)

Ingredients

1	¼-ounce envelope (7 g) gelatin	¾	pound cream cheese
¾	cup orange juice	1	tablespoon lemon juice
¾	cup sugar	½	cup whipping cream
¼	teaspoon salt	1⅛	cups canned pumpkin
3	eggs, separated	½	teaspoon ground cloves
1	teaspoon vanilla	½	teaspoon ginger

Method

Soften the gelatin in ¼ cup orange juice. Heat the balance of the juice with sugar, salt, and gelatin mixture and stir until gelatin is dissolved. Add beaten egg yolks, which have been warmed with some of the juice. Cook, stirring constantly, until slightly thickened. Add vanilla. Whip together cream cheese and lemon juice. Add gelatin mixture. Chill until thick as jam. Whip cream. Fold pumpkin, spices, whipped cream and stiffly beaten egg whites into gelatin mixture. Pour into a 10½-inch springform pan. Chill.

Pear Tart

This recipe by Giuliano Bugialli is presented exactly as it was dictated by him in class in Florence. If you have a favorite pastry, use it instead, but do follow his ideas about crockery bowls for the sauce and other such hints. They're rooted in cooking history and quite valid today. (Serves 8)

Ingredients

Crust

1½	cups unbleached, all-purpose flour	1	tablespoon granulated sugar
			Pinch of salt
½	cup sweet butter	1–2	tablespoons cold water

Filling

4	Bosc pears, ripe	½	cup granulated sugar
3	cups dry red wine		Small piece of lemon peel
¼	cup port		Pinch of cinnamon

Pastry Cream

4	egg yolks	1	cup cold milk
6	tablespoons granulated sugar		Small piece of lemon peel
3	tablespoons potato or corn-starch	2	pounds (approximately) dried beans for shaping pastry shell

Method

Crust

Sift the flour onto a board. Arrange flour in a mound. Cut butter into pieces and place them over the mound. Let rest for ½ hour. Start mixing the flour into the butter with your fingers until almost all the flour has been incorporated. Then make a well and put in the sugar, salt and water. Start with 1 tablespoon of water and after mixing, add more if needed to obtain a very smooth and elastic dough. Wrap the dough in a dry towel and refrigerate for at least 1 hour.

Filling

Peel, core and cut the pears into quarters. Place a saucepan on medium heat with wine, port, sugar and lemon peel. When the wine reaches the boiling point, add the cut pears and sprinkle on a pinch of cinnamon. Let simmer for about 15 minutes, then transfer the pears with a slotted spoon to a crockery bowl and let cool completely. Reduce the wine mixture until a syrup is formed (about 20 minutes), then transfer the syrup to another crockery bowl. There will be ⅓ cup syrup or less.

Pastry Cream

Mix egg yolks in a bowl. Add the sugar and beat well until light. Add the starch and beat until thick. Add the milk, then transfer to the top of a double boiler which is placed over hot (not boiling) water. It should not touch the water. Add lemon peel. Stir continuously over the hot water until mixture is thick enough to coat a spoon, or, as Bugialli says, until it "cries one tear." Transfer pastry cream to a crockery bowl and let stand until cold.

Preheat the oven to 375°F. Butter a 10 inch × 1¼ inch pie plate. Unwrap the dough and knead it for 1 minute on a board. Flour the board, then using a rolling pin, roll out dough to a thickness of ¼ inch. Roll layer of dough on rolling pin and unroll it over the buttered pie plate. Gently press down the layer of dough to bottom of the plate. With a knife cut around the top to remove the overlapping pastry. Fit a sheet of wax paper or aluminum foil loosely over the pastry, then put all the dried beans in the plate to keep shape of the shell while baking. Place the plate in the oven for about 40 minutes. Remove the plate and lift out the paper containing the beans. Let the crust rest for about 15 minutes.

Assembly

Place a layer of poached pears in the pie shell, pour the syrup over and then the pastry cream. Place in the oven for another 15 minutes, then remove and let rest until cold.

Short Order Cooks

Two 14-ounce cans (398 mL) of pear halves in syrup can be substituted for fresh pears. Drain the pears. Reserve syrup. Place a saucepan on medium heat. Measure in reserved pear syrup and add sufficient dry red wine to make 3 cups. Add ¼ cup port, a small piece of lemon peel and a pinch of cinnamon. When the wine syrup reaches the boiling point, add the drained pears and a sprinkling of cinnamon. Simmer for about 5 minutes. Continue with original recipe.

When a recipe calls for egg yolks only, what should I do with the egg whites?
Add them to scrambled eggs or omelettes or poach them and use them in sandwich fillings. If you wish to freeze them, place each white in an ice cube tray, freeze, remove and store in a freezer bag. Allow to come to room temperature before whipping. Defrost whites in the refrigerator. Or use them up in Fresh Fruit Meringue (p. 125), Chocolate Nut Meringue Torte (p. 142), Filbert Meringue Bars (p. 118), Strawberry Soufflé (p. 130), Grand Marnier Soufflé (p. 131), Rhubarb Meringue Flan (p. 121), and Fish Soufflé (p. 54).

Zabaglione Mousse

Whenever my culinary ambitions soar, I whip up a zabaglione for dessert. But traditional zabaglione must be made and served immediately so my guests either must remain at the table without me or all troop into the kitchen to watch. This particular zabaglione can be made ahead, in fact it has to be, and for this reason it has supplanted my traditional recipe. It's rich—but so good. Serve it after a special dinner. (Serves 6)

Ingredients

6	egg yolks		1	pint whipping cream
7	tablespoons sugar		4	ounces semisweet chocolate
8	tablespoons dry Marsala			squares cut into small cubes

Method

Cream the egg yolks and the sugar until lemon colored and fluffy. Add the Marsala. Put into a double boiler placed over hot (not boiling) water, and continue beating with a wire whisk until the mixture is whipped enough to hold a small peak. Let cool. Whip the cream and fold into the egg mixture. Then fold in the chocolate bits and refrigerate in a glass bowl until serving time. May be frozen.

Zabaglione Cream

Here is a Florentine variation on zabaglione using rum. It should be prepared ahead and served very cold. A delightful finish to a festive meal. (Serves 8)

Ingredients

5	egg yolks		$\frac{1}{2}$	cup dry Marsala
5	tablespoons granulated sugar		$\frac{1}{4}$	cup white rum

Whipped Cream

1	pint heavy cream		1	teaspoon icing sugar
2	tablespoons granulated sugar			

Method

Put water in the bottom of a double boiler and set on the heat. Place the egg yolks in a bowl and add the sugar. Stir with a wooden spoon, always in the same direction, until sugar is completely incorporated and the egg yolks turn a lighter color. Add the Marsala and rum slowly, mixing steadily, then transfer the contents of the bowl to the top of the double boiler. When the water at the bottom is boiling insert the top part. Stir with a wooden spoon, moving in the same direction. Just before boiling, the zabaglione should be thick enough to stick to the wooden spoon. It is ready. Do not allow it to boil. Remove the top part of the double boiler from the heat, stir contents for 2 or 3 minutes more, then transfer to a crockery bowl to cool about 1 hour. When the zabaglione is cold, prepare the whipped cream. Whip with sugar until very stiff, gently fold in the zabaglione. Mix carefully but thoroughly with a whisk. Cover bowl with aluminum foil and place in refrigerator until needed.

Brandy Alexander Mousse

I am grateful to Crispin's restaurant in Toronto for this dessert! (Serves 6)

Ingredients

1	¼-ounce envelope (7.0 g) unflavored gelatin	¼	cup brandy
½	cup water	1	cup heavy cream, 18% butter-fat
3	eggs, separated	¼	cup crème de cacao
⅔	cup sugar		Nutmeg, grated
	Salt		

Method

Sprinkle gelatin on top of cold water and let stand until softened, about 3 minutes. Beat egg yolks, slowly adding ⅓ cup sugar and pinch of salt. Add to gelatin mixture and place over low heat, stirring constantly until slightly thickened, about 5 minutes. Remove from heat and let cool slightly. Stir in brandy and crème de cacao and chill until mixture mounds slightly. Meanwhile, beat egg whites with ⅓ cup sugar until very stiff. Set aside. Beat heavy cream until very stiff. Set aside. Fold gelatin mixture into the beaten egg whites, then fold into whipped cream. Place in serving dish and chill. Just before serving, sprinkle mousse with grated nutmeg.

Prepare gelatin in sm. bowl
Beat yolks c ⅓ c sugar   Beat egg whites
Add gelatin   Beat cream

Chocolate Mousse

In French, the word *mousse* means a 'froth' or a 'foam.' It is the frothy texture of the mousse which distinguishes it from a pudding. There are many recipes for chocolate mousse, some incorporating whipped cream and some calling for egg whites only instead of whole eggs. Here is a classical version which can double as a chocolate soufflé. As a cold mousse or hot soufflé, it is excellent served with vanilla- or rum-flavored whipped cream.

I first saw this recipe in the magazine *Pleasures of Cooking*, which specializes in dishes for the food processor, and discovered that chocolate fanciers and expert cooks favor this method. If you have a food processor here's your chance to let 'er rip! You can make this in the traditional way—simply melt the chocolate carefully and slowly, then fold it into the beaten yolks and sugar, season and fold with the whites of eggs.

If a chocolate dessert has been refrigerated, remember to bring it back to room temperature—or thereabouts—so that the flavor will mellow. (Serves 8–10)

Ingredients

6 ounces unsweetened chocolate, broken into pieces	¼ teaspoon cream of tartar
1 cup sugar, divided in half	2 tablespoons strong coffee (or 1 teaspoon instant coffee dissolved in 2 tablespoons hot water)
⅓ cup water	
6 large eggs, at room temperature, separated	1 tablespoon vanilla extract

Method

Cut chocolate pieces in half and place in work bowl of food processor fitted with steel blade. Process ON/OFF, ON/OFF a few times, then process 1 minute or more, until chocolate is very finely chopped. Dissolve ½ cup sugar in water and bring to a rolling boil. With the machine running, pour boiling mixture through feed tube and process until smooth. Let mixture stand in processor. Beat egg whites with cream of tartar until firm, either by hand in a large bowl, or with electric mixer. Then add remaining ½ cup sugar gradually, beating until stiff peaks form.

Add egg yolks, coffee and vanilla to cooled chocolate mixture. Turn machine ON/OFF. Scrape down sides. Let machine run 3–4 seconds. Add ¼ of the egg whites and process, turning machine ON/OFF, until well mixed. Add remaining egg whites all at once. Turn machine ON/OFF only until the chocolate mixture starts to cover the egg whites. Do not overprocess. If large clumps of egg white remain, gently fold them in with a spatula. It does not matter if mixture has streaks of egg white. Spoon mixture into 9 individual ½-cup serving dishes or a 1½-quart serving dish. Refrigerate several hours until firm.

For a baked soufflé, spoon mixture into 10 individual 6-ounce custard cups, filling them ⅔ full. Place filled cups on an aluminum baking sheet in a preheated 425°F oven. Bake for 12–15 minutes or until well puffed. Serve immediately.

Chocolate-Coated Fruit

What can I say about this dessert? It's delicious! A word of caution—dampness is the enemy of chocolate so be sure the fruit is well dried.

Ingredients

6	ounces semisweet or bitter-sweet chocolate	Styrofoam and toothpicks
2	pints strawberries, fresh cherries, apricots (dry), seedless tangerine slices	

Method

Melt the chocolate in the top of a double-boiler. Water below should not touch bottom of pan above. Remove from heat leaving chocolate over the hot water. *Brush* dirt off strawberries; pick up a strawberry by the green stem, dip half into the warm chocolate, drain excess coating, stick toothpick into strawberry and place on styrofoam to dry.

Notes
1. Don't dip fruits on a very hot day; humidity will prevent the chocolate from hardening.
2. Choose fruits that are perfect—bruises will cause moisture to leak through.
3. Do not store the dipped fruits in the fridge, they will turn grey-brown and sweat.
4. Reheat dipping chocolate if it becomes too cool.
5. To coat raspberries, lay, open side up, on a cookie sheet, on which melted chocolate has been poured. Cut or break to serve.
6. Use a medical syringe and fill with grand marnier. Inject into the fruit centre.
7. This recipe works best when fruit is dipped approximately 2 hours ahead of serving time.

Chocolate Pots of Cream

Luckily, I'm not a chocoholic or the day I spent with New York chocolate specialist Nan Mabon at the Culinary Centre would have finished me! This dessert is most attractive served in small china serving dishes, although Nan used champagne flutes and they were elegant. This is rich so you might like to make the servings small. It's a good last-minute dessert. Do be careful to wait until the dessert is cool before covering with plastic wrap, otherwise the steam will condense and cause brown spots on the surface. (Serves 6–8)

Ingredients

8 ounces chocolate, sweet, semi-sweet or bittersweet	2 cups light cream (10%)
	6 egg yolks

Optional

½ cup heavy cream, whipped	Candied violets

Method

Break up or coarsely chop the chocolate. Place it with the cream in a small, heavy saucepan on moderate heat. Stir frequently with a small wire whisk until the chocolate is melted and the mixture comes to a boil. Reduce heat and simmer, stirring, for about 3 minutes. In a small bowl, stir the yolks slightly just to mix. Very gradually, add the hot chocolate mixture to the yolks in a thin stream, stirring constantly with the whisk. Pour into a pitcher and then pour into individual dishes. Cool and refrigerate covered. To serve, top each with a rosette of whipped cream and a bit of candied violet.

Mocha Hazelnut Torte

Torte means 'not very much flour at all.' This torte lives up to its name as a rich, chocolate-flavored dessert. Slice it thinly. It's filling. (Serves 8)

Ingredients

4 ounces unsweetened chocolate	1 tablespoon sweet butter, softened
3 tablespoons sweet butter, softened to room temperature	1 3-ounce (85 g) bar coffee-flavored milk chocolate
3 eggs, separated, yolks well beaten	1 3-ounce (85 g) bar bitter-sweet chocolate
2 tablespoons all-purpose flour	½ cup chopped nuts (optional)
½ cup sugar	
⅔ cup hazelnut praline (following)	

Hazelnut Praline
½ cup blanched toasted hazelnuts   1   teaspoon lemon juice
½ cup sugar

Method

Preheat oven to 350°F. Butter a 7 inch × 3 inch × 3 inch or a 9-inch round pan and dust with sugar; shake out the excess. Melt the chocolate for the cake in the top of a double boiler and remove from heat. Slowly beat in the softened butter, the yolks, flour and sugar. Beat the whites until they form stiff peaks, stir one tablespoon into the chocolate mixture then gently fold in the rest of the whites. Pour into the prepared pan and bake on the middle shelf of the oven for 35 minutes (5 minutes less for the round pan). Place pan on a cake rack to cool.

Praline

Toast the hazelnuts carefully. They should be barely brown and your nose will tell you first if they are done. As the smell of roasting nuts wafts from the oven, they should be turning brown. Turn them into a clean tea towel and wrap. They'll steam cook in the towel. Then roll them between your fingers. The skins should be left behind. This can be done weeks in advance and the nuts stored in an airtight jar in the refrigerator or freezer.

Combine sugar and lemon juice in a heavy skillet. Melt over low heat, stirring constantly with a wooden spoon. When a deep, golden color has been obtained and the sugar is dissolved completely, stir in the toasted nuts. Quickly pour out onto a well-oiled cookie sheet. Let harden; then pound in a mortar or grind in a food processor until praline reaches the consistency of crumbs—do not make a powder. Then, mix the praline with the softened butter.

Melt the two chocolate bars for the icing in the top of a double boiler. Edge around the cooled cake with a knife and turn it out of the pan, onto a cool tea towel. Hold the tea towel over the pan, invert and it comes out cleanly. Carefully slice cake in half, lengthwise, and trim edges of layers if necessary. Spread the bottom layer with the hazelnut praline out to the edge. Transfer onto a serving platter and place strips of waxed paper just under the edges of the cake. Put top layer in place. Carefully spread chocolate icing around sides of cake and smooth remainder over the top. Remove waxed paper strips. Carefully decorate sides and top of torte with chopped nuts.

Chocolate-Nut Meringue Torte

Here is a crisp chocolate dessert that can be made one day and served the next. Be careful not to fill the layers too far ahead of time as the cake will turn soggy. Store the meringue layers in the cooled oven or at room temperature. It's best made in the winter as meringue will not remain crisp and dry in humid summer weather. Bake the meringue on Friday, whip the cream on Saturday—and serve! (Serves 8)

Ingredients

6 1-ounce squares semisweet chocolate	1½ cups chopped walnuts
6 large egg whites	3 cups heavy cream
½ teaspoon cream of tartar	¼ cup icing sugar
1½ cups sugar	3 tablespoons Crème de Cacao, Tia Maria or other coffee liqueur
2 teaspoons vanilla	
½ teaspoon almond extract	

Garnish

Unsweetened chocolate curls

Method

Preheat oven to 300°F. Melt chocolate in the top of a double boiler. Set aside to cool. In a large bowl beat egg whites until frothy, add cream of tartar and continue to beat until the whites hold soft peaks. Gradually beat in sugar. Beat the meringue until it is smooth and glossy. Add vanilla and almond extract. Stir ¼ of the meringue into the chocolate, fold the chocolate mixture into the remaining meringue gently but thoroughly and fold in the nuts. Trace 3 circles, 9–10 inches in diameter onto sheets of buttered foil which have been arranged on 3 baking sheets. Divide the meringue among the circles, smooth evenly with a spatula, and bake in the middle of the oven for 30 minutes. Let the layers remain in the oven until cool. In a chilled large bowl beat heavy cream with the icing sugar and coffee liqueur until it holds stiff peaks. Trim the meringue layers into even rounds, reserving the trimmings. Put 1 of the layers on a serving plate, spread it with ⅓ of the cream mixture and sprinkle with ½ the reserved trimmings. Add another meringue layer, spread it with another ⅓ cream mixture, and sprinkle the top with the remaining trimmings. Add the last meringue layer, spread with the remaining ⅓ cream mixture and garnish the torte with unsweetened chocolate curls.

Chocolate Decadence

Mary Risley tells me that this dessert swept California dining rooms in 1980. It is rich and gooey and chocolate lovers swarm to it. (Serves 12)

Ingredients

Cake

8	eggs	2	tablespoons flour
2	teaspoons sugar		Cocoa, unsweetened
2	pounds semisweet chocolate	1	cup heavy cream

Raspberry Sauce

2	10-ounce (283 g) packages frozen raspberries	Sugar to taste

Method

Preheat oven to 400°F. Line the bottom of an 8-inch springform pan with parchment paper. Break the eggs into mixmaster bowl and set over hot water. Stir the eggs with the sugar until they are warm. Beat until thick, pale lemon in color and the consistency of whipped cream. Carefully fold in the chocolate, melted and cooled, with the flour. Pour 3/4 of the mixture into the prepared pan and bake 15 minutes. Cool, unmold, refrigerate overnight, or freeze for later use. The remaining 1/4 batter can be baked in the same manner in a small pan, chilled and formed into decorative balls. Use a teaspoon to shape the balls, roll them in unsweetened cocoa and chill.

To decorate the cake, whip the cream until stiff enough to hold peaks. With an 8- or 9-inch flexible metal spatula cover the cake with 3/4 of the cream. Place the rest in a pastry bag with a star tube. Make rosettes around the top of the cake and place a chocolate truffle on each rosette. Serve with raspberry sauce on the side.

Raspberry Sauce

Thaw and drain frozen raspberries. Purée in a blender, run through a sieve and sweeten to taste.

Et Cetera

Cranberry Sauce
(Makes 1 quart)

Ingredients

1¾ cups sugar
1 cup water
¼ cup orange juice

4 cups cranberries, rinsed and picked over
2 teaspoons orange rind, grated

Method

Combine the sugar, water and orange juice in an enamel or stainless steel saucepan. Bring to a boil over low heat and simmer 5 minutes. Add the cranberries and cook the mixture over moderately high heat for 4–5 minutes, or until berries have popped. Stir in orange rind. Let the sauce cool and chill it.

Pig and Plow Mustard

Ingredients

½ cup dry mustard
½ cup sugar
¼ cup vegetable oil

¼ cup horseradish
¼ cup cider vinegar

Method

Mix together the mustard and sugar. Stir in the vegetable oil, horseradish and cider vinegar and mix until you have a smooth blend. Spoon into small jars and cover with plastic wrap and lids. Store at room temperature. Allow 3 months for flavors to mellow.

Hiker's Special
Just the thing for backpacking or school lunches. Eat it as you do granola.
(Makes 3½ cups)

Ingredients

½ cup raisins
⅓ cup candied pineapple pieces
½ cup dried apple slices
½ cup whole almonds

½ cup filberts
½ cup peanuts
½ cup pumpkin seeds

Method

Combine all ingredients in a large bowl, toss well to blend. Store in tightly covered container.

Raspberry Mint Jam

Did I name this recipe in jest? That raspberries cost a mint, there's no doubt; however, this is not how the title originated. It was, in fact, more inspired. I was casting about for a flavor that might heighten the raspberries' sweet richness when my eyes happened to light on the mint in the garden. Once tried, it became a part of my repertoire for years. As prices rose, my gifts of raspberry mint jam became even more appreciated. I love to give gifts of food, particularly one that is so rare as homemade raspberry jam. (Makes 7 1-cup jars)

Ingredients

10	cups raspberries (approximately 5 pints)	¼	cup lemon juice
			Handful fresh mint
8	cups sugar	¼	cup Crème de Menthe liqueur

Method

Set aside 2½ hours of uninterrupted time. Wash and dry the jelly jars, making sure that there are enough lids and sealers. Sterilize the jars. (See note following recipe.) Have wax ready for melting. Wash and examine the raspberries. Discard any berries that have soft or bruised spots. Drain and measure.

Choose a deep pot for cooking the jam. Avoid copper, as it holds the heat too well and could allow the jam to overcook. Place the fruit, sugar and lemon juice in the pan and turn on the heat. Allow to cook uncovered. Bring to the boil and continue to boil for 20–30 minutes. Stir constantly all this time.

As final temperatures vary considerably, depending upon the fruit and pan size, I can give an approximate time only. It must be tested. Remove pot from the heat, place a bit of jam on a cold plate that has been stored in the freezer. Chill it immediately for 1 minute in the refrigerator. Your jam is ready when the chilled jam on the plate wrinkles if pushed with a finger. You can use a candy thermometer to help indicate when jam is done. Most fruits reach the jam stage at 220°F. Some fruits high in pectin (gooseberries, black currants, Damson plums) reach the jam stage slightly earlier—218°F.

When the jam is done, add mint and liqueur and ladle it carefully into sterilized jars, leaving ¼ inch headspace. Wipe any drips from the inside rim with a cheesecloth-wrapped fork. Any drips can hinder the proper seal. Cool the jam slightly, then pour a layer of hot melted wax over the jam, rotating the jar so that the wax will adhere to the glass to form a close seal. Leave until hardened, add a second layer of melted wax, again rotating the jar. Cover and store in a cool place. Label with name and date.

To Sterilize Jars

Oven Method
Set clean jars on rack in oven. Heat to 225°F for at least 10 minutes. Remove from oven when needed, allowing to cool slightly.

Boiling Water Method
Cover the washed jars with hot water inside a large kettle or invert them in 1–2 inches of water. Bring to the boil and continue to boil for 15 minutes. Leave in hot water until needed.

Low-Calorie Strawberry Jam

Large amounts of sugar are the preserving agents in jam. When a low-sugar jam is required, the preserving effect is lost. That is why frozen jam is popular with dieters. Artificial sweetener can be used without much loss of texture. While it hardly can replace a natural homemade jam, this version has helped many a dieter face breakfast.

Ingredients

5	cups strawberries	1	tablespoon lemon juice
1	2-ounce (56 g) package pectin crystals (Certo)	3½	teaspoons artificial sweetener

Method

Crush the berries using a blender, food processor or by hand. Add pectin and lemon juice. Bring to the boil and boil for *exactly* 1 minute. Remove from the heat and add sweetener, stirring. Continue for 2 minutes. Pour into small freezer containers, cover and freeze. Thaw to use. Always store in the refrigerator.

Apple Mint Chutney

Ingredients

1	large cooking apple	1½	tablespoons fresh mint, chopped
2	tablespoons apricot jam		Salt and pepper
1	tablespoon cider vinegar		

Method

Peel and grate the flesh of the apple. Mix at once with jam, vinegar and mint. Season with salt and pepper to taste. It should be both sharp and sweet. Bottle in sterilized jar.

Brandied Cranberry Applesauce

This colorful sauce is a perfect accent for pork, fowl or ham. It's equally good with hot or cold meats. (Makes 5 cups)

Ingredients

6 medium apples, peeled, cored and coarsely chopped	½ teaspoon cinnamon
1½ cups fresh or frozen cranberries	⅛ teaspoon ground cloves
¾ cup maple syrup or honey	¼ cup brandy
	¼ cup chopped pecans (optional)

Method

Combine apples, cranberries, syrup, cinnamon and cloves in a 4-quart saucepan or Dutch oven. Bring to a boil over medium-high heat. Reduce heat, cover and cook for 25 minutes, stirring occasionally. Uncover and continue to cook about 5 minutes more. Stir in brandy, sprinkle with pecans. Serve warm or cold.

Chinese Plum Sauce

An original and authentic-tasting plum sauce to use with Chinese food. Make some when the pumpkins are in season. (Makes 1 cup)

Ingredients

¼ cup cooked, mashed pumpkin	Juice and rind of 1 lemon
¼ cup vinegar	¼ teaspoon black ground pepper
¼ cup water	2 tablespoons cornstarch
1 cup sugar	¼ cup water

Method

Combine pumpkin (use canned, if you have it) with vinegar, water, sugar, lemon rind and juice, and pepper. Bring to a rolling boil over high heat in a small saucepan. Stir constantly. Mix cornstarch and water together. Add to the hot liquid and continue cooking and stirring until it thickens and there is no longer a taste of raw cornstarch—about 4 minutes. Let cool and use as a sauce for egg rolls or spareribs or in recipes calling for commercial plum sauce.

Glazed Raisinola

Another granola with lots of raisins. (Makes 6 cups)

Ingredients

2	cups rolled oats	1/4	cup slivered almonds
1	cup shredded coconut	1/2	cup butter
1/2	cup wheat germ	1/4	cup honey
1/2	cup sunflower seeds	1	cup raisins

Method

Preheat oven to 300°F. In a large bowl combine first 5 ingredients. In small saucepan melt butter with honey. Pour over dry mixture, combining well. Spread mixture on greased baking sheet and bake for 30 minutes, or until golden brown, stirring several times. Remove from oven and add raisins while still hot. Cool completely, store in tightly covered container.

Poppy Seed Candy

Purim, the Jewish festival that celebrates Queen Esther's deliverance of the Jewish people, is famous for poppy seed specialities, perhaps because they were favored by Queen Esther herself. Here is a traditional sweet for Purim. (Makes 12 candies)

Ingredients

1/2	cup honey	1/2	cup ground nuts, almonds, walnuts or hazelnuts
1/4	cup sugar		
3/4	cup poppy seeds	1/3	cup slivered almonds

Method

Blend the honey and sugar together in a heavy saucepan over low heat until the sugar dissolves. Add poppy seeds, bring to the boil and keep cooking over low heat until 250°F is reached on a candy thermometer. (It will pass from the stage where a ball of candy held between the fingers will retain its shape but not flatten unless pressed to the firm ball stage where the candy is more rigid but still not caramelized and hard.) It should take about 10 minutes to reach this stage. Add the ground nuts and cook for a minute longer.

Pour into a greased, lightly buttered, 8-inch square baking dish. Sprinkle the almonds overtop. Work quickly now. Dip a sharp knife into warm water and cut the candies into 12 squares. Remove to a serving dish.

Index

Methuen
0-458-95180-3